Planning by Futuring, Futuring as Planning

Planning by Futuring, Futuring as Planning

Using Your Futures Mindset to Develop Social Media Policy

Richard Bernato

ROWMAN & LITTLEFIELD
Lanham • Boulder • New York • London

Published by Rowman & Littlefield
An imprint of The Rowman & Littlefield Publishing Group, Inc.
4501 Forbes Boulevard, Suite 200, Lanham, Maryland 20706
www.rowman.com

6 Tinworth Street, London SE11 5AL, United Kingdom

Copyright © 2021 by Richard Bernato

All rights reserved. No part of this book may be reproduced in any form or by any electronic or mechanical means, including information storage and retrieval systems, without written permission from the publisher, except by a reviewer who may quote passages in a review.

British Library Cataloguing in Publication Information Available

Library of Congress Cataloging-in-Publication Data Available
ISBN 978-1-4758-3807-7 (cloth)
ISBN 978-1-4758-3808-4 (pbk.)
ISBN 978-1-4758-3809-1 (electronic)

Frank and Helen Bernato, my parents, were not educated people. The times and circumstances never enabled them to pursue what they certainly had the capacity to be in the "outside" world. But that didn't prevent them from always striving to provide my sister and me with all of what they could give us to seek *who we* had the capacity to be. That included sacrifice and support we can only imagine. It is to them that I dedicate this book, because from them, I learned the themes of capacity, hard work, and vision.

Contents

Preface ix

1 Introduction: The Tower of Twitter 1

2 Weaving Futures-Based Change Leadership with Transformative Engagement with Developing Social Media Policy in Schools 9

3 Futuring I: Setting Up for a Preferred Future, Creating the Right Conditions to Establish Committed, Coalesced Purpose 19

4 Futuring I Continued: From Content to Purpose to Process 27

5 Processing to Purpose: Organic over Inorganic Every Time 35

6 Futuring II: Future Wheeling the Future 45

7 Futuring II Continued: Cross Impact Futuring 55

8 Creating Scenarios 65

9 A Futures-Based Process in Place: Action Design 75

References 89
About the Author 91

Preface

Planning by Futuring, Futuring as Planning: Using Your Futures Mindset to Develop Social Media Policy suggests policy formulation processes about social media as an emerging, if not already "present" future for every school or district.

For sure, clearly, in many senses this future has already arrived. School districts and buildings pressed to formulate policies that "regulate" its usage among students, and perhaps "encourage or discourage" its use as an instructional strategy bundle, are challenged to consider the possible, and probable, let alone the preferable futures for which they must prepare.

The fact that this book is "frozen" in the time when it is published in a certain sense renders it behind the times. This topic and research and or ideas about the themes and issues it suggests will have already passed the curious reader by, for if there was ever a time that practice precedes research, empirical or anecdotal, it is in the use of social media in education.

Instead, this book's greatest value, insofar as this topic is concerned, is that our "solving" for it—i.e., the very process of engaging stakeholders in deep consideration, purposing, analysis, creative problem-solving, and futuring toward a preferable one in which I have embedded the topic—has the true worth for leaders committed to continuous change process.

Nonetheless, here I will briefly offer some themes the latest research suggests. You will find these issues implied and reckoned with among the case study dialogue and debriefings within the text. These are:

- Practice precedes the research.
- There is a lack of consensus regarding policy.
- Policy formulation benefits from deep engagement.
- A framework for impact has value.

PRACTICE PRECEDES THE RESEARCH

Despite the fact that social media usage in all its forms and venues continues to embed itself, for better or worse, in ways that had not been forecast, research about its impact on educational leadership policy remains murky.

I find this curious but not altogether surprising when it comes to educational practice. Innovation rarely comes without birthing pains to our institution. One reason for that is the reactive, rather than its opposite, nature to leadership mindset. All too often, educators tend to forget that their institution is embedded in the "world out there" until it is too late to prepare for its impact.

In general, since its practices evolved organically and without direction until we realized that there was a *need* for direction, only now have some research concepts begun to solidify.

THERE IS A LACK OF CONSENSUS REGARDING POLICY

Otchie and Pedaste (2020), in a metanalysis of literature, cite Manca and Ranieri's observation that there is little consensus about social media's role in teaching and learning. This, despite the fact that its usage has the capacity to support constructivist concepts of interactivity, engagement, and knowledge building.

Their analysis extracted several themes for further inquiry:

- Collaboration
- Communication

- Interaction
- Information dissemination
- Entertainment
- Teaching, learning, and resource sharing
- Socialization

Clearly these have value for exemplary thinking and learning and as clearly, these require the futures-based leader to seek to embed them in her school organizational culture. And yet, despite their obvious benefits, the authors conclude that policies about social media's usage and support for its integration into instruction remains slow at best. Perhaps this is because, while the "social" in social media is obvious enough, instructional strategies in making it part of the teachers' toolkit are inconsistent to date.

POLICY FORMULATION BENEFITS FROM DEEP ENGAGEMENT

Muls et al. (2019) attribute schools' difficulty in defining their own role in its usage a cause for the need to use deep engagement in creating policy. This is especially true insofar as the extent to which social media impacts students' attitudes, and especially their behavior. Legal ramifications are certainly in the mix.

More significantly, Ying, (2013) describes social media policy as a "hot potato" but also recognized that creating policy creates the opportunity for both deep and wide engagement, not only of internal stakeholders but also of parents and community. This recognition of the cross-systems networks of those who should be engaged can be engaged in co-designing significant change.

A FRAMEWORK FOR IMPACT HAS VALUE

Synthesized, the message seems clear: to explore, support, and solidify opportunities to combine social media's capacity to activate engagement among students with its ability to provide motivating and constructivist-laden skills and content. Do this carefully, but do it. Do it carefully by grounding it from a futures-based leadership perspective so that how it is embedded in instructional–cultural practices reflects collective and purposeful input from a cross-section of all stakeholders.

Using a framework, like that advocated in this book, will enable futures change leaders to create unique communities of reform.

Planning by Futuring, Futuring as Planning: Using Your Futures Mindset to Develop Social Media Policy is certainly first and foremost meant to offer a case study format to recognize how the futuring process, together with the synthesis of theories and themes that it embodies, can be used to develop policy for sustained futures-based change.

Indeed, the process demonstrated can be applied to a multitude of emerging futures that thought educators must consider. And there are certainly plenty of those that could benefit from the deep processes this book demonstrates.

Questions about education, how we deliver it, how we *organize to* deliver it, how we judge *whether* we deliver it effectively, persist, despite our perception that we are doing the best we can at making "it" effective. Age-old points of view rebound off each other as the latest "crisis" erupts about whether we are "doing" it effectively at all. Some questions might include:

- To what extent do we have a collective commitment to what we believe education's purpose is in the first place?
- To what extent does a public-school-system philosophy have the capacity to meet the cross talk of perceived purposes?
- In striving to be all things to all people, do we fail to effectively meet any purpose?
- Does our public school system *drive* our societal priorities and needs or *react* to them?
- What can it be?
- What *should* it be?

In addition to the matter of futuring for effective development of social media policy, it cannot be ignored that as of this writing, the current COVID-19 crisis, whose yet unresolved effects cut across virtually all dimensions of our society in ways many people had not anticipated, has pressed education, once again, to the front of many dialogues. The furor has its own share of dimensions. I would term them as symptomatic rather than as root cause themes.

For example, questions about whether to open schools at all, to open in some sort of hybrid online/face-to-face combination, or to return to in-class learning five days a week fail to squeeze the elephant out of the room—that is, that school leadership and policy makers failed to future. Failing to future is a euphemism for neglecting to think long-term, for overlooking possibilities and probabilities, for not keeping the purported purpose(s) before them, for leadership inadequacy, if not incompetency.

That the competencies, skill sets, and dispositions necessary to position a school district to align its purposes with its basic beliefs are not part of their leadership practices mantra, corrals the schools they lead to reactive, rather than proactive positions. This notion suggests root cause issues that are likely either in conflict with the school's deepest beliefs or have been terribly, if not impossibly distorted amid the flurry of emergencies and short-term needs that corrupt their decision making.

Objective attempts to distill the root causes to explain this general failure may range from complacency or lack of commitment to their beliefs to weakness of will to take the stances and make the decisions that may be politically unpopular, to the inability to read the signals of their emerging futures, or to a misunderstanding of the administrators' charge to lead as well as to manage.

However, in the light of the very serious issues the pandemic has suggested, this book can also support the school leader who seeks to embed a futures-based change leadership philosophy into her culture in two ways: The first is to be able to future for or away from probable futures that have or shortly will affect your school: e.g., the pandemic, online or hybrid instruction, etc.

The second, and more valuable process it provides is a *toolkit* for transforming your school via a coalesced-collaborative think tank of your stakeholders into a flattened hierarchy approach. Doing so will enable you to co-empower your colleagues to work with you, to future with you, and to not only narrow down possible, probable, and preferable futures, but to also nurture a mindset toward what Amy Webb in her book *The Signals Are Talking,* (2016) calls the *Projected Future.*

Her notion of a Projected Future does not speak about just-around-the-corner technology developments. Projected Futures are ten, twenty, thirty years, and more down the line. These may be developments suggested by the convergence of today's trends in technology, demographic changes, and economic models. However, as Diamandis and Kotler point out in *The Future Is Happening Faster Than You Think* (2020), they are on their way. These are futures that will depend on school districts to have created systems to anticipate their emergence. These are school districts that have embedded creative thinking, collaborative leadership, and learning organization disciplines into their culture's capacity to change. These are schools that have used forecasting processes and have valued futures-based can-do dispositions prepared to influence change. Thus, whether it be flying cars, artificially intelligent textbooks, pandemics, an economic downturn, global unrest, climate emergencies, or the emergence of social media, the "healthy" futures-based school system will be prepared for it.

Richard Bernato, EdD
2020

Chapter One

Introduction

The Tower of Twitter

The famous Genesis story tells how the ancients decided to work together to build a tower to the heavens in the city of Babel. Whether the goal was to prove that they had the ability to do such a thing is a subject for biblical scholars to consider. We do know that the Bible tells us that God chose to ensure they would not be able to do this. Some versions recount how He destroyed the tower. Others go further by saying how He destroyed their ability to communicate, and thereby obstructed the builders' ability to collaborate toward a common purpose by creating different languages and cultures so they were unable to work together.

On the one hand, an interpretation of their failure might be a consequence of their hubris to presume they could do such a thing in the first place. On the other, the story could be interpreted as an explanation for the diversity of cultures, ethics, values, and beliefs that reflect the mosaic of our world.

Somewhere in here lies an analogy for how organizations might characterize its use or non-use of Twitter, Facebook, and other social media technologies. Are their uses examples of attempts to build a virtual tower to heaven knows what? Is the dissonance of crosstalk, misinformation, half-truths, unilateral pronouncements, and exchange of trivia that often characterize social media exchanges, examples of a Tower of Babel punishment by the heavens to show how misguided our presumption is that we actually have the mass collaboration skills that are suited toward common purpose?

What is the state of the Tower of Twitter in many school organizations? Is social media's usage prohibited or severely restricted for fear of unforeseen consequences? Is social media's capacity to influence poorly understood? Is there a Tower of Babel–discordance among stakeholders who seek to use social media that obstructs unanimity of purpose?

Or, is social media becoming a vital part of the communication and professional development efforts of the organization? Do professional staff identify and exchange sources of learning and strategies for their colleagues to consider for their own practices? Are virtual communities of practice established where staff collaborate among participants to use dialoguing and focusing-down techniques so that they can generate new ideas, problem-solve issues of common concern, and seek personal mastery? To what extent are parents and students engaged in the array of exchanges that social media's usage generates?

In other words, have school leaders and their stakeholders taken the time to align their policies and organizational practices with social media's capacity to catalyze, empower, and transform its organization on the whole, and its stakeholders as individuals? Have they used futures-based change leaders' competencies, skills, and dispositions to create their preferred future?

Current research appears mixed. One reason for the small body of empirical material may be that in some cases practice precedes research. Since social media's usage is a rapidly evolving phenomenon, research about it simply has not had the time to catch up to it. In addition, the effects of social media's usage in schools are compounded by who the beneficiaries, or the victims, of its implementation are. Children and their learning are not variables to be taken lightly, and school leaders understandably are often justifiably leery of turning social media loose in their schools.

Planning by Futuring, Futuring as Planning: Using Your Futures Mindset to Develop Social Media Policy is *not* a book intended to convince the reader of all the capacities that social media's promise might have for school improvement. Instead, this book assumes that social media does have the potential to be a major tool in the arsenal of enabling schools to enact their system-wide change efforts.

However, this notion also requires that futuring social media into a school's practices be understood for the extent to which it can have a meaningful impact on generating transformative participants' high engagement. Consider this backward scenario:

SCENARIO: A BACKWARD HISTORY OF DISTRICT XYZ IN THE YEAR 2030

Teacher Jones walked into the faculty room. She hadn't been in there since last month. In fact, she only came to the actual brick-and-mortar building that used to house the children of ABC School, monthly. Indeed, the children only actually attended the school on a biweekly basis, mostly for socialization and intervention services and to check in with their Project Leader Teacher, who worked with them individually and in small groups, to develop and master their community-based projects. The balance of their schooling was done in online small learning groups, where they interacted through their Mentor.

She was always amused at what the faculty room seemed to represent. There were couches, coffee machines, and refrigerators, study carrels, even a small professional library of actual physical books and magazines. There were some dinosaur-like desktop computers and printers, too. Instead of the interactive bulletin boards some schools had, ABC still had old-fashioned corkboards and pushpins for attaching notices and memos.

Yet she was pleased that there was a place for her to go to meet her colleagues face-to-face. There was something to be said for these kinds of places, where professionals could inspire and commiserate with each other, could exchange ideas, and support each other's creativity to fashion in-person and online activities for their students.

It was even more comforting to realize that while the physical faculty room still continued to serve as a forum for professional growth and inspiration, the school stakeholders, after several fits and starts these past years, had settled on its fundamental purposes: i.e., to shed old habits of thinking, and to presence a collective will to find new ways to support, create, and inspire each other—in other words, to maximize transformative high engagement behaviors, in order to do the same for their students.

That this was largely now done through organic and inorganic professional development practices that had been nurtured by a sophisticated use of social media platforms and dialogue strategies had been no easy feat. It had taken careful futuring. for sure.

As a mid-career teacher, she could trace how the school—indeed, most schools now—had taken this trail:

Last year, in 2029, it seemed to finally gel into a systemic practice that had been grounded in the near-universal assertion that ABC School was committed to developing students' capacity to meet their own emerging future by ensuring that the school's cultural beliefs had been transformed by using social media to help drive capacity. And that careful use of futuring and design-thinking skills, active, and inquiry-based dialogue exchanges had catalyzed the staff to change their assumptions about how they could steer to a collective preferred future.

About three years prior, there had been spirited reaction against the design plan the Strategic Planning Council had generated in 2020. This had happened in spite of the SPC's best intentions to engender total group commitment to use social media as an exchange of information, best practices, problem-solving strategies, and personal professional development.

Those who objected did not do so out of a rejection of the universal recognition that their school needed to renew its organizational structure and practices. What had bothered them was that the implementation of the new practices seemed uneven and that the plan in place had set its professional development targets without considering the readiness stages of individual teachers.

Luckily, the plan had also called for regular formative "check-ins" of each goal and their associated strategies' progress. As the feedback was valid, the group took great pains to adjust by distilling the root causes at play, determining whether these issues aligned with the basic beliefs and values of their school culture, and designing additional strategies to bring teachers along at their pace and capacity.

In 2022, a communications "crisis" of sorts threatened the plan's energy and intent. While it is often taken for granted that stakeholders know how to listen to, respond, and engage in group conversations, the opposite is often true. A "cyber-conversation," in which colleagues interacted in a variety of social media venues, often asynchronously, and posted varieties of information of varying quality, had turned out to be very difficult to bring to purposeful and effective closure. Jones smiled when she thought about how teachers had begun to question these activities' quality and doubt whether all this was wasted energy. She was pleased, though, when the SPC decided to slow down the implementation in order to pilot the process more thoroughly and to devote much more energy to professional development of inquiry, dialoguing skills, and critical evaluation of data that colleagues would post for exchange and analysis.

In 2021, the plan had solidified. School leaders had involved its teachers in researching various social media platforms. The school's Strategic Planning Council had made a critical decision to neither standardize which social media platform everyone might use nor require a given technology device. They had based their decision on the belief that teachers' uses of both would eventually sort out the optimum platforms and would help generate the direction the whole initiative would take. Jones remembered being troubled by this decision at the time, but she had been generally pleased about how it had evolved.

The year 2019 had been Smith's first year in teaching. She remembered scarcely understanding all of what she had to do in order to meet her students' needs. However, it had quickly become apparent that the school then had been a victim to its failure to change along many fronts, and this had resulted in a school culture that was devoid of morale, directionless, and in need of a psychic commitment to change its instructional and organizational practices.

Although more a witness to, rather than a leader of, the grassroots efforts of the school community to turn the school around, Jones had become a willing supporter of its efforts by joining committees and informal groups to consider what they all needed to do.

The district endorsed a steering committee, later called the Strategic Planning Council, that embraced the formula—i.e., futures-based leadership is a consequence of the school's capacity to change; a school's capacity to change consisted of the extent to which it practiced; and systems' disciplines, with presenced, purposeful thinking and collaborative leadership. In addition, the belief had become that a school's capacity to change success was dependent on the extent to which it embraced futuring skills and self-empowerment dispositions.

That committee would begin its work in earnest to design a plan in which teachers and leaders would empower each other to seek new ways to move the school forward. A major part of this was a plan to encourage systemwide use of social media to inform, exchange, and motivate its participants to take meaningful and purposeful actions.

The offered scenario is meant to serve three purposes. It offers some of the issues, themes, and concerns that any school organization must future for in order to maximize the value of the energy it has invested to leverage any necessary change. On another hand, the story is this book's first foray into showing the reader how a futuring skill, in this case, a Backward History strategy, enables stakeholders to sharpen their likelihood to shape their preferable futures.

Most importantly, the scenario is meant to demonstrate how the futured implementation of social media had become a vehicle to transform the engagement, not only of Ms. Jones, but also that of her colleagues from one direction to many—from one plane to many, from inorganic to organic—as the exchanges and interactivity derived from social media, positively transformed the nature of the collective and individual energies of the staff and educational community.

Transformative High Engagement implies a different kind of energy and is relevant because there are events, experience sets, and interactions that impel individuals and groups to shed old ways of thinking in favor of new ways to interpret their realities. The results can be both the self-empowerment and the co-energizing of like-minded individuals toward efforts and purposed actions they may not have realized lay within them. Hence, proper and futured fostering of social media's influences can serve as a tool in the arsenal of comprehensive organizational change.

Otto Scharmer noted, "Energy follows attention. Wherever you place your attention, that is where the energy of the system will go. 'Energy follows attention' means that we need to shift our attention from what we are trying to avoid to what we want to bring into reality" (https://www.presencing.com/principles). This concept suggests a shift in how organizations may see how they function, and it intersects with La Loux's exploration of how organizations, including schooling (2014), may evolve to maximize their energies toward their presenced purpose.

This presenced purpose, which is grounded to a preferred future, captures the desire to collectively catalyze and inspire a school's individuals, which intersects with Transformative High Engagement's nature. Of itself however, Transformative High Engagement cannot be considered an isolated variable.

Transformative High Engagement is about promoting those behaviors, dispositions, and actions that more nearly ensure that a group can crystallize its collective vision and actions most effectively. Stakeholders do not need social media to practice High Engagement. However properly futured, social media, infused by Transformative High Engagement, can create profoundly powerful and effective group action.

Social media, in the context of understanding its role in school improvement, is about the cyber-exchange of information, opinions, and conclusions that will contribute to potential actions *or inactions*, both of the individual and of the group/participant exchange that takes place. The product of these commutative factors results in collective, purposive, and positive action. This is called Collective Purpose.

Please note that an additional factor undergirds the system offered to ensure its effectiveness. That factor has been alluded to throughout this chapter, and it is Futuring, where the success of the interaction between social media usage and Transformative High Engagement is dependent on how the Futures-Based Change Leader, as described in *Futures Based Change Leadership: A Formula for Sustained Change Capacity* (Bernato 2017) uses the competencies and skills of futuring to ensure that the implementation of a change initiative like social media will yield the kind of transformation that serves the school's students best.

Therefore, this book's purpose, depicted largely through a fictional case study format, will show how the factors of Collective Purpose, Social Media, Transformative High Engagement, and Futuring Practices are related to a culture disposed to continuous innovation. More specifically, this book will demonstrate how to use Types I, II, and III Futuring Practices to ensure social media's capacity to influence positive change.

ISSUES TO CONSIDER

To what extent does your school/organization:

- Enjoy a culture that has engrained the capacity to change in its beliefs, assumptions, values, and practices?

- Enjoy a culture where behaviors and attitudes exist where stakeholders and subgroups experience transformative high engagement?
- Enjoy a culture where collective purposeful and positive actions are the rule rather than the exception?
- Routinely exhibit attitudes and dispositions where people believe they can take actions to influence a preferable future in alignment with their purpose and vision?
- Have the skills and competencies to inquire, think about, and use futuring skills to do this?
- Know the state of the Tower of Twitter in their school?
- Know how to embed social media skills of dialogue, exchange, and inquiry into their beliefs and practices to foster positive actions?

ESSENTIAL POINTS

- The purpose of this chapter is to lay out the issues associated with social media insofar as they weave with Transformative High Engagement, Collective Purpose, and Futuring.
- Social media appears to have the capacity to have considerable influence on group and individual behavior.
- Social media's influence in transforming school cultural practices is a trend that must be explored.
- Four themes will guide the conversation in this book.
  - Collective Purpose
  - Transformative High Engagement
  - Social Media
  - Futuring Practices and Dispositions
- The book will concentrate on helping readers practice and master the dispositions and skills of futures-based planning to properly acculturate a school's beliefs and practices across several chapters that will be sustainable and effective.

Chapter Two

Weaving Futures-Based Change Leadership with Transformative Engagement with Developing Social Media Policy in Schools

Principal Smith was exasperated. He didn't like when he didn't have his arms around the whole elephant before he made a decision. In this case, not only was this elephant still moving, but he hadn't gotten any rein at all on its direction within the confines of his leadership world. Pretty difficult to make a decision, establish policy, and implement it when the animal in the room was having none of that.

His technology director, Carol, wasn't making it any easier. Neither was her obvious "co-conspirator," Ellen, the English department chair. Both were advocating that he should challenge longstanding policy about using social media in instruction.

Carol continued the debate. "Dr. Smith, I never watched the show. It was before I was born. And I don't think you watched it, either. But we all—you, Ellen, and I—have heard of *The Flintstones*."

Actually, as a child, he had watched reruns of the cartoon series about a Stone Age family's adventures. But he was sure that Ellen and Carol, much younger than he, might never have seen an actual episode. That didn't matter. What Ellen was implying, he was certain, was that her mindset was more nearly grounded in the past than it was in the future. He didn't like the implication, even if it was partially true. As principal, he was the person responsible for enforcing policy in the high school. He was the one who saw the ripple consequences of what his most respected and competent administrators were advocating.

The principal offered, "Why don't I bring in Mike so he can tell you what his Mondays are like as a result of what you would like to see happen during the school day? I have an assistant principal whose entire Monday is about tracking down rumors, threats, and cyberbullying that took place in a hundred parties, school sporting events, and virtually anyplace two teenage students found a reason to say something to or about one another, every weekend. That didn't count their parents, who also used social media to spread their own versions of reality, all at odds with someone else's version of reality, not to mention also at odds with *actual reality*. And he and I must intervene to clear this away every week. You want me to support that?"

Carol and Ellen answered in unison, "Yes!"

Ellen continued, "We don't endorse that negative energy at all. You know that. But it's time to leverage the power of the engagement energies social media promise so that we can re-create how we lead each other to learn."

The principal sighed. "Okay, English chair, what was that old English proverb?"

Ellen smiled. "Yes, yes, 'The road to hell is…'"

"…'paved with good intentions,' the principal added. "Okay, let's figure out how to future for this before we rush in where angels may fear to tread."

Principal Smith's challenge—indeed, any leader's challenge is to:

- *consider the prospect* of an organization's change;
- do so in *the context of its mission and purpose;*
- *assess its capacity* to adapt to, or transform from, the probable future that change will likely effect,
- *evolve how to build* a coalesced, collaborative process to generate direction for the collective energy that must follow, in order to
- *create a Preferred Future.*

While these steps suggest a linear strategies-set, meant to embed the capacity of social media into his staff's instructional culture, Principal Smith must not think of this undertaking as a mechanistic recipe. Both the leadership competencies, and the dispositions welded with these skills, require a deft blend of organic, instead of inorganic leadership, best characterized by Futures-Based Change Leadership (Bernato, 2017).

Bernato's book *Futures-Based Change Leadership* argued for a blend of premises and practices that are necessary for an organization to generate and sustain deep, purpose-based changes for alignment with the needs of the Emerging Future (Scharmer, 2014). These begin with assessing the extent to which the organization's capacity to change incorporates three elements. The first is *Providing for Learning Organization Principles*. Another element is *Engraining a Design-Thinking/Idea-Generating Array of Creative Thinking Processes* into their routine decision making, and a third is *Using Collaborative Leadership Principles* to fuse the above into a culture with the ability to both fluidly design for and sustain an organic transformation of their practices.

Here, Senge's premise of a Learning Organization (2106) provides the directional frame for recognizing that a school, like any organization, is obligated to weave five practices—he called them Disciplines—to ensure that the "being" that is the school, will continuously reinvent itself in order to survive. These reinventing energies must align with the needs of the Emerging Future lest the organization fail to serve its purpose.

Design Thinking is a notion that intersects with Senge's Learning Organization findings. Design thinking emphasizes the use of creative problem-solving processes that weld left-brain, problem-framing techniques with an array of right-brain creativity, idea-generating, and fluency techniques. This cultural practice yields solutions that might not ordinarily have been considered or created at all. That organizations, especially schools, neglect to emphasize creative thinking strategies amounts to leaving many of their best ideas on the floor because their decision-solution-structure mindset does little to nurture the approach.

Neither Learning Organization nor Idea-Generating practices can flourish without a third dimension, Collaborative Leadership Principles. Senge's five disciplines—i.e., positive mental models, attention to personal mastery, using team learning skills, committing to shared vision, and having the structured ability to recognize subsystems relationships—require the organizational theme of sharing leadership contributions throughout the whole of the Learning Organization. In like manner, the very idea of creating fluent, flexible, and elaborative ideas is dependent on the whole to acculturate these across their organizational leadership capacities.

As we consider Principal Smith's task—i.e., to future a change in instructional practices that is complemented by the power of social media—we can see the importance of each of these dimensions in her school's cultural capacity to change in the first place.

His school as a Learning Organization, without the disciplines-health described above, will not be able to form the constructs for long-term change implementation. His school, without the ability to think creatively, to conjure new solutions to problems of action and practice, will not be able to meet the future that Principal Smith, Carol, and Ellen collectively fancy. His school, unable to defeat the "Tower of Babel" I-thinks that plague collective school leadership and collaborative attempts, will tumble upon itself.

Even if these dimensions are more or less in place, according to Bernato, there is another factor whose strength will deeply affect Smith's school's capacity to change. In other words, these cultural capacities to change are not enough of themselves. The principle of using Futuring strategies and processes, with their attendant dispositions, is critical to ensure that his school can birth and nurture the change.

Consider the term *futuring* as a noun, a verb, and a gerund. The reader will find the word *futuring* spread throughout this book and used in a variety of ways. On the whole, it is meant to suggest the act of forecasting among three kinds of futures: what is Possible, what is more nearly Probable, and what is Preferable. *Futuring* is an umbrella term for strategies and processes, complemented by futures-based dispositions, and therefore will be the process applied to most of Principal Smith's and his staff's efforts. Here, we see that a thoughtful alchemy of forecasting, parsing, planning, and comparing against the organization's value yardsticks will acculturate a school to identify their most probable, emerging futures. More importantly, they will be able to determine the extent to which their likely futures align with what they want to happen.

In the case of embedding social media into instructional practices, we can see that conceiving, shaping, nurturing, and upgrading this "new tower's" future, as it twists, turns, and evolves on the one hand, is a beneficiary of a stakeholder culture with futuring DNA, and on the other, is interdependent with the three-dimensional cultural capacity features described above.

The intersection of these dimensions will also organically generate a High Engagement culture whose benefits will have much to do with transforming each participant's investment.

Let us now return to Principal Smith and his ABC High School by understanding the backdrop of his school and of his students in order to use that school as the basis for using futuring to drive social media into ABC High School's instructional culture.

Visualize a typical ABC High School student first.

Norman Student rightfully thought of himself as a fair student, but certainly no valedictorian. He thought of himself as pretty average for what he also thought was a pretty average town. He was beginning to get the idea, as he entered his junior year, that he had to pay more attention to his world and to his local surroundings than he had bothered to do till now. He and his friends had begun to share opinions about the world they were getting ready to enter, and they had readily agreed that it wasn't a friendly place. More than that, they and he had begun to realize that they weren't terribly prepared well for it.

Norman had a job, in the local warehouse store. It didn't ask too much of him except to move boxes around, sweep floors, and help customers. He could see that the store was successful. Indeed, it had contributed to the rapid desertion of local stores on Main Street that could not match their prices. He could also see that there were only so many positions in the company to which he could ever aspire. Add in the fact that he wasn't terribly interested in doing that in the first place.

Yes, the town and his school were certainly changing. A lot of kids in the school had trouble speaking English. The teachers were a mixed lot of dedication and of quality. Some of them were hardworking and creative, but many seemed disillusioned and were not trying either to be interesting or to help him and his friends master new technology, or even learn good vocational skills they could use to work some place.

He guessed he was going to college or maybe a career training school. But he knew that the sense of dissatisfaction he had with his young life was somehow connected to a school that didn't meet his or his community's needs.

Norman is High School ABC, and the information below will help us recognize how future-based leadership principles may help his school transform.

ABC High School isn't any different from most American high schools. It is located about fifty miles from a major urban center whose trending sprawl has changed the area to be more nearly suburban than rural. Economically, blue collar/lower middle-class citizens dominate the population in the district's northern sector. These individuals are a mix of folks whose families have lived here for several generations, and of more newly arrived families who have fled the city to the west for an affordable house, a backyard, and a garage. A sizeable portion of new residents have moved into converted summer bungalows for permanent living opportunities in an area that they consider affordable.

ABC's demographics have changed in similar ways to its region. Once homogeneously white, its population has begun to see increasing numbers of Latino and African American populations. A large portion of each of these groups has come here for the same reasons that previous district residents have come. That is, to have affordable and desirable housing for their children in a good district. However, the ravages of a nasty recession have also brought residents to the district that have economic and social, not to mention language problems among the Latino population, and these have challenged the school's resources.

Academic expectations on the surface are strong; however, they sometimes suffer in economic priority to these. Its academic achievement performance compares favorably to its surrounding districts. However, none of these districts are particularly noteworthy for extraordinary academic achievement in terms of the customary yardsticks, like percentage of students taking Advanced Placement courses, entering four-year colleges, Intel Science winners, and the like.

Perhaps this is best exemplified by the fact that while most ABC High School graduates go to community college and four-year college programs, many graduates do not complete their degrees and largely return to the area to seek jobs in local industrial park enterprises or in the growing but low-paying service sector.

After an uncommon length of time for school district principals to lead any district, ABC's principal finally decided to retire. The school board had a general idea that they wanted a new leader who could rejuvenate the high school programs and even upgrade them. They perceived their students' need to be academically competitive in the overall emerging economy of the area. At the same time, plagued by the nation's slow emergence out of a crippling recession, they knew they could not "kill the goose that lays the golden egg" by significantly raising the tax rate. In other words, it was a matter of "doing more with less."

Enter Principal John Smith, who took the position at ABC after a successful tenure in a smaller local school district. The Board charged him with a full review of ABC High School services and programs and with recommending new leadership initiatives. He realized the infusion of social media technology into teachers' instructional arsenal might be part of these recommendations.

He also realized that his school's students have not performed well in the required standardized examinations. He knew there were many reasons for this. He knew he had to lead his leaders to re-create a school that assured a quality, high-standard of dispositions, skills, and twenty-first-century competencies, but how could they do this so it would work, and so that it would last?

He has considered the many variables that may affect his desire to do this.

ECONOMIC AND DEMOGRAPHIC STRESSORS

Smith realized that the world had changed, and those changes impacted how his district should educate children. He also realized that the school's demographic changes had become another stressor for it. As with most of the region, new immigrants, especially Latino children, had entered the district. He was concerned when she noted to her administrators that Latino students' performance lagged far behind their counterparts, something they seemed to accept without conversation.

TEACHERS' AND ADMINISTRATORS' CAPACITY TO CHANGE

He considered his own perception of the extent to which his staff, both teachers and administrators, was prepared for the changes before them. He was also aware that most calls for change among both his teachers and administrators were met with a mixture of fear, disdain, and resistance. He had tried to isolate the factors that supported these feelings, and he worried mightily about their capacity to do this. These issues were at the mercy of:

- their own psychological capacity to change;
- the extent to which the change expectations were clearly communicated and understood by them;
- their preparation as teachers and as administrators;
- their motivation to change; and
- the present system's capacity tools to help make change sustained.

His initial interviews with administrative staff had also led him to several concerns. He felt that his administrators on a whole had great interpersonal skills and had used these well to maintain what is. However, their mastery of engaging staff in using data and in collectively generating meaningful plans and actions on students' behalf was clearly wanting. He had also found out that the premise of identifying the roots of cultural and systemic issues that drove their schools' practices was rarely if ever even considered let alone put in motion.

Most importantly, he'd realized that their future-based skills to both anticipate the emerging future and to plan for or against it just did not exist. He thought there were probably two reasons for this. The first was the leadership style and expectations of the last principal. While generally well-meaning, he had operated out of a political frame more than anything else and used a unilateral approach to most decisions. The result was that his administrative staff usually operated out of the same frame and moreover never felt especially empowered to think anything other than what the principal told them to think.

The other reason was that they had neither ever been trained to use data sources to develop long-range planning, nor did they know how to engage stakeholders in appropriate collaborative decision-making, except for perhaps simple and fleeting window dressing occasions.

BOARD/ADMINISTRATION/UNION ADVERSARIAL RELATIONSHIP

From what he has been able to determine, the ABC teachers' union's adversarial stance to most leadership initiatives had its roots in the heavy-handed way that administrators had traditionally treated them. Apparently, this had mollified over time but knee-jerk us-versus-them and them-versus-us typically characterized the dynamics between the two. Recent developments have only exacerbated the longstanding tension. Increased federal regulation, most notably that of NCLB and now Race to the Top pressures, have been interpreted as unrealistic and inflexible attempts to reform schooling. ABC administrators, unskilled at implementing change, and wary of these same expectations, have clumsily put these into place.

PARENT DISPLEASURE

Caught in the push-pull between administrator and teacher union mud-wrestling are the parents of some one thousand children in the ABC School. While some contribute mightily to the typical parent-teacher association activities, and most attend extracurricular and athletic events, they, too, have been buffeted by media negativity about teachers and their own discontent about to what extent ABC has done the best by their own children.

In the end, he theorized, he needed to enable her leadership and his staff with a combination of systems thinking, collaborative leadership skills, and change process competencies that would be also be grounded in a futures-based-planning mindset. Doing so had at least two cautions. The first was time. The second was the ABC systems' and stakeholders' inability to cocreate sustainable change.

He was very aware that all too often, change initiatives do not get the time to do what must be done to not only reform or re-create the systems needed to sustain what they have started. Educators, policy-makers, and parents more often than not do not have the patience to stay the course and will Ping-Pong between what is currently in place to the latest holy grail. This is usually a function of the capacity of the organization's stakeholders', professional, parental, and political skills to knit the new into the organization's fabric.

The sum of ABC appears to consist of dissatisfaction, concern, disagreement, conflicting agendas, and an inability to collaborate to coalesce a common purpose. It is compounded by its victimhood to national and global factors that shape both policy and attitudes. These intertwine with the challenges of ABC. And so, he concluded, these require a different kind of leadership, an alchemical leadership, to engage their common emerging futures to either make decisions to adapt to these or to take actions to transform their district into something altogether new.

The unexpected urgency that his chairs, Ellen and Carol, had brought to her desk presented the opportunity to begin the process. That it is about social media is as much about its metaphorical symbolism of twenty-first-century change expectations and obligations as it is about the issues associated, both positive and negative, with its implementation into the instructional culture of ABC High School.

"Hmm," he thought, "if we can do this well, we can do most anything." He smiled. "But we'd better get it right the first time, because if we don't, there won't be a second time."

ISSUES TO CONSIDER

To what extent does your school organization:

- Have the culture's capacity to initiate, create, implement, and sustain organizational change?
- Have the ability to factor both internal and community/world factors into realizing their emerging future insofar as social media may be involved?
- Have the skills to create a preferred future?

ESSENTIAL POINTS

1. The processes, both organic and inorganic, require a combination of deft use of Learning Organization disciplines as exemplified by Peter Senge, creative thinking and reimagining as exemplified by Otto Scharmer's Theory U, and Design Thinking themes.
2. Collaborative Leadership Practices are essential, as well.
3. These are dependent on the school's leadership and/or school improvement think-tank team's mastery of futures forecasting skills they do not customarily practice, in tandem with a clear understanding of their common dispositions toward the future and change.

Chapter Three

Futuring I

Setting Up for a Preferred Future, Creating the Right Conditions to Establish Committed, Coalesced Purpose

Smith turned to Mike, his assistant principal, and to Carol and Ellen. He opened by saying, "All right. Mike, Carol, Ellen, and I have been having long conversations about social media."

Mike groaned. "The bane of my leadership existence," he said, then smiled. "Carol, what have you and your colleague been corrupting our leader about?"

Ellen was ready for that. "Mike, Dr. Smith has already helped us understand how hard you have worked to deal with the tension, bullying, rumors, and other disturbing issues that are generated by how students misuse social media and how this impacts their emotional and physical health."

Carol added, "We certainly understand that and respect how hard you work to minimize the negative results of these misuses."

Mike was appreciative. "Thanks, I do the best I can, with the help of our mental health staff, to clear away as much as I can so that teachers can teach with a minimum of negative energy. Teaching is tough enough." He went on, "But thankfully, my head isn't too far in the sand. I realize that social media has the capacity, when used properly, to add whole new dimensions to how we think and learn."

"That is what we think we need to harness here at ABC," said Dr. Smith. "Our school can serve our students, help them become part of a future that may be passing them by if we don't seek new ways to help them learn. Carol and Ellen claim that social media can be part of our changes."

He went on, "I have to confess that my own personal jury is out about whether or how we should address this potential new initiative. So, we need to help each other construct a process that, first of all, engages a cross-section of ABC High School stakeholders."

Mike added, "And gives them objective information to enable them to develop a deep, common, and coalesced purpose. If we can set the structure to get this done, it may help us decide the best ways to make this happen."

Ellen agreed, but with some doubt. "To a man with a hammer, every problem is a nail. Are you using the dreaded 'committee' word?"

Smith was frustrated, but he understood her skepticism. Smith was very aware that ABC High School had its share of committees, but he also knew that these groups, while well-meaning, had rarely accomplished anything significant. Ellen's furrowed brow certainly reflected that point of view. But Smith also believed that committees, when properly empowered and properly trained in processing data and in distilling their implications, can be vibrant idea machines.

"Well, yes, I guess I am. I'm at a loss about any other way to embed a massive change mindset into our practices without finding every way possible to keep everyone involved in as many ways as possible. Can you suggest any other strategy?" he asked.

Carol spoke up. "I think you're right, Dr. Smith. But you won't have to listen to the groaning in the faculty room when the word goes out that you're trying to begin another committee. Your union friends will oil up their resistance machine right quick."

"I'll deal with that," Smith said. "And frankly, I honor their skepticism. The only way to turn their frown upside down is to invest futured intent, support, and training into *growing* that group into a meaningful, effective one, whose energies, recommendations, and actions have real value."

Ellen was impressed. "Okay, what should we call this committee?"

Mike smiled. "We can call it 'The Committee to Enter the Twenty-First Century.' The CE21C."

Smith offered, "How about the SPC, the Strategic Planning Council?"

Carol reacted, "The word *strategic* puts me off a bit. Even if we are actually developing a process that will become 'strategic.' Can I suggest 'Futures Forward Instruction Group'? If you think about it, once we get a dialogue generated, we will be talking about social media for sure, but my money is that the dialogue will morph into the deeper and wider idea of innovative instruction, richly purposed and embedded in uses of technology, not as the end in itself, but as the means to align with a series of purpose-based transformations. That is, after all, what we need to do at ABC."

Mike whistled. "Well, that's a mouthful. But that's what we are talking about! I like the FFIG!"

A COLLABORATIVE MINDSET THAT HIGHLIGHTS ENGAGEMENT PRINCIPLES

A "problem" with change is that it is rarely a linear process. To the contrary, change is not tidy. In fact, as we recall the themes of capacity to change in chapter 2, we are reminded that capacity often benefits from organic rather than inorganic thinking, that is a product of collaborative, often "unscripted" exchange, among engaged participants.

Futures-Based Change Leaders use precepts of Design Thinking and Creative Problem Solving to recognize that creativity has four components. These are fluency, flexibility, elaboration, and originality. Fluency connotes idea generating and is best understood by brainstorming techniques. Flexibility speaks to the evolution of creative thought where contributors realize that an initially offered idea can be mixed with, shortened to, expanded by, or twisted into new idea shapes. Elaboration challenges creative thinkers to flesh out ideas that appear to have imaginative value. And originality is the final piece where idea(s) appear to be something no one might have developed without having been fluent, flexible, and elaborative in the first place.

The critical adjunct to Principal Smith and his staff's thinking is that the tenor of their conversation is clearly collaborative. Together, they have commingled ideas and energies to create a sense of common reality where the sum is greater than the total of its parts. Their collaboration, born of enthusiasm and mutual respect, enables fluid thinkers to create something new.

We also find evidence of systems thinking, especially of team learning, mental models, and a budding sense of shared vision. These undergird the quality of their creation.

At this point, as we consider the conversation among Dr. Smith, Mike, Carol, and Ellen, we can see how the exchange among them has enabled the issues social media's instructional uses may suggest, and of consideration of how its potential to enrich teaching and learning may evolve. The group has begun to coalesce into an ad hoc think tank that is planning how they might engage the ABC learning community in visiting the initiative. But what can we expect next?

Smith smiled. "Okay, FFIG it is."

Ellen also smiled. "And now I am thinking of the Humphrey Bogart movie where he said, 'round up the usual suspects.'"

"Well, I'm encouraged," said the principal. "At least we've moved past cartoon characters, and no, *Casablanca* was before my time, too. But you raise a tricky question—two, actually. The first is how to attract stakeholders with the potential to coalesce into a productive think tank. The second is to realize that the word you just dropped into the conversation is the missing ingredient to transform their capacity into something they weren't before."

"Now you're using phrases that are foreign to us, Dr. Smith. Not sure what you mean."

Mike offered, "You said 'futurist.' Is that what you're pointing out, Dr. Smith?"

The light went on for Carol, and before Dr. Smith could answer, Carol said, "Yes, futurist! You are creating a group of educational futurists, thinkers who use information and creative thinking to forecast the future!"

Smith was pleased. "Yes, exactly. And actually, there is another word that I didn't use but also applies: *alchemy*. You know, those so-called scientists in the Middle Ages who sought to transform lead into gold. *We* want to transform our FFIG Futurists into alchemists who are charged with transforming how we might use social media in our instructional practices."

"But," he went on, "there is no Philosopher's Stone to help us do this. We are going to have to convert our own thinking and actions to sow the acorns that will enable us to be FFIG Futurists."

"Not sure what you mean, Dr. Smith," said his assistant principal.

He looked at the group. "To what extent do you believe that none of us is as smart as all of us?"

Ellen, Carol, and Mike looked at each other. Carol spoke up. "The answer seems so obvious that I am guessing I am wrong. Yes, I believe that is true."

Smith waited for the others to weigh in. "Looks like you all agree with that statement. It sounds true. Yet is it, really? Can we think of groups we've been part of, or have seen that, in fact, weren't very smart together at all?"

Mike said, "Okay, for sure, I have seen some jury decisions and some election results I have questioned. So, you're saying that none of us is as smart as all of us, unless we know how to be smart together."

"I am. And that means that we have to think carefully about what we know, what we don't know, and what we don't know that we don't know, to frame our purpose and analytically recognize what we need to know to make the right decisions and recommendations."

That is when Mike offered, "So we have to choose and choose carefully."

Ellen clapped. "More movie trivia by which we guide our actions. But I am back to now rounding up the right suspects."

This segment helps us understand how the principal's group begins to coalesce toward purpose. But more importantly, it also accents the recognition that the change they seek to consider extends beyond social media for social media's sake. Rather, the change they seek is more nearly about transforming the whole that is ABC High School.

In addition, Smith has not only introduced the notion of futuring to the process but has also helped them understand that a group that, in their case, may hold multiple college degrees and expertise still may not be able to be effective without the presence of High Engagement variables (Wohlstetter, 1994). Groups typically will either fail from the start or over time, if the following variables are not present.

They begin with Power Boundaries. This concept affirms that a group must know its charge limitations and authority before it begins its work. Failing to do so causes confusion and resentment if its recommendations are not taken up seriously by formal leadership.

Knowledge is the next critical component. It has two subsets. The first is knowledge about and mastery of the processes and inner workings of the systems and issues they are analyzing. Without this experience, groups will often fail because their noble intent is diluted by their inability to truly address relevant issues.

The second subset of Knowledge is Human Relations. While group members may be very bright people with the necessary mastery of experiences and processes that help the group function effectively, they may, Tower of Babel–like, nonetheless crumble because the structure has not accounted for the matter of human relations necessary to coalesce. If they don't have the interpersonal skills to be cohesive, the group cannot succeed.

The third variable is Information, and that, too, has two subsets. The first subset is data, both quantitative and qualitative. These forms of data, from a variety of sources, must be available to the group members in order for them to use their Knowledge skills to distill the most objective themes that lie beneath and that await their reasoned identification. Decisions absent all the appropriate information amount to hunch choices rather than futured ones.

Connected to the Information dimension is the idea of input and communication. Deliberations, tentative issues, and decisions must be distributed to all stakeholders for their response and input. In turn, their input must be delivered to the group so that these points of view are considered before closure on decision actions and recommendations. Failing to do so invites needless discontent by exclusion.

Goals are the fourth variable. The FFIG must either be given or have the authority to create goals that are SMART. Energy will follow direction when direction is identified.

Distributed Leadership is the fifth variable. If Dr. Smith seeks to empower his school's stakeholders, he needs to take pains to ensure that, where opportunity is appropriate, to assign responsibility to individuals to perform vital but short-term tasks, possibly leading smaller subgroups of the whole FFIG, and even more optimally, including stakeholders with relevant experience who are not standing FFIG members.

Resources are next. These are what they sound like. Typically, groups will connect this concept with money. Often that is the case. However, it is also important to realize that an engaged group may need more supports than money for success. These include time, expertise, and commitment to their tasks.

The least-powerful variable to more nearly ensure High Engagement is rewards. This is particularly true in school systems or other nonprofit organizations. In contrast, rewards may have more influence in private corporations where individuals may be recognized and rewarded for their efforts by bonuses, raises, and promotions. Nonprofits, on the other hand, are rewarded by intrinsic satisfaction, which may have longer-lasting value than extrinsic incentives.

The nascent FFIG then has begun to consider these factors in order to ensure that it will have the sustainable capacity to meet its mission. Yet there is more to consider, and Mike frames the issue well for "The Right People on the Bus" (Collins, 2001).

Mike responded to Ellen, "If by 'the usual suspects,' you mean we need to enlist, draft, or drag the best people we can find to be FFIG members, we all certainly agree with you. A book I read a few years ago, *Good to Great* by Jim Collins (2001), offered a now well-known phrase, 'the right people on the bus.' Clearly you're talking to the same point."

Ellen nodded. "Yes, and this is a tricky chemistry. It's easy to reach out to teachers, staff members, and typically involved community and business leaders. It's not so easy to be certain that we are 'hiring' their willingness to serve welded with our expectation that their input will always be what we want to hear."

"But it's another thing to get the balance of objectivity, creativity, and evenhandedness that we need," said Linda. "That is very important."

"Throw in what I call the 'I' word," added Mike. "We need to be certain of their ability to Influence their peers and/or the people whom they represent."

"I will offer two more 'I' words, their Independence, and their ability to solicit Input from their peers, as well," said Ellen. "We really don't need yes-men. We need folks who will say the emperor wears no clothes when that is accurate. And we have to rely on them to include, wherever they can, others' points of view, as well as help them understand the thoughts behind our eventual actual recommendations."

Linda smiled. "Well, I can think of over four hundred people in Washington I'd leave off our FFIG and a large section of our own community. But we can do this."

ISSUES TO CONSIDER

To what extent does your school organization:

- Have a research-based system for enlisting and formulating effective stakeholder teams?

- Realize the issues associated with high engagement in effective decision-making and planning-design teams?
- Recognize that the evolution of a group is not necessarily linear?
- Select group members by carefully acknowledging members' roles, their talents, and allow for a cross-section of points of view.

ESSENTIAL POINTS

High Engagement variables of an effective stakeholder group include themes like:

- Power boundaries
- Knowledge skills to crunch the issues and purposes at hand
- Interpersonal skills
- Sufficient data, both quantitative and qualitative, to make informed conclusions and plans
- Provisions for disseminating decisions and deliberations to all constituents for their information and input
- SMART goals
- Provisions for distributing leadership responsibilities as appropriate
- Resources, both financial, time, expertise, and intent, to meet the purpose

Chapter Four

Futuring I Continued

From Content to Purpose to Process

THE RIGHT PEOPLE

Mike referred to his clipboard. "This looks like the final list. The last person to agree to our request was Ulysses. He asked a lot of questions, and I did my best to answer them."

Smith sighed. "I'm sure you did. The union president was playing his adversary role, I'm sure. It's what he does best. On the other hand, as Ellen said, we can't have twenty people all agreeing the sky is green if it isn't."

"He'll be fine," Carol said. "As you pointed out, it will be healthy for the group to use a variety of perspectives to get to yes, whatever yes will mean."

"That may be the most difficult part of what we are generating, at least at the outset," offered Ellen. "Getting to a common lens sometimes gets overlooked when a new group is being born. And we will need a common lens to gather as much information as possible, to distill it, and to agree to common purpose."

Mike returned to his clipboard and handed out a copy of the membership sheet. "Okay, it was good that at least two of us were present every time we interviewed those who volunteered and those we drafted."

Smith smiled. "'Drafted' is such a harsh verb, Mike. How about we call it 'solicited'?"

Mike returned the grin. "Oh yes, of course, 'solicited,' a rose by any other name."

"It was wise, too, to ask the various stakeholder organizations' heads for names of potential members to represent their groups," said Carol.

"For sure. We validated their connection to us and showed that we honored their participation," agreed Ellen.

"And when I convene the group's first meeting, I'll make sure they understand their responsibilities to get and give input from their communication with their colleagues," said Dr. Smith. "In addition, I will spell out their charge very specifically, as well as have them understand how they will come to closure on whatever recommendations they will generate."

"Okay, that is a great point, Dr. Smith. How will we know that the FFIG has agreed to offer a recommendation? And, by the way, are they recommending, or are they deciding our school's direction insofar as using social media in our schools?"

HIGH ENGAGEMENT ISSUES

Dr. Smith and his think tank are methodically moving through aspects of the High Engagement Model described in chapter 3. More specifically, the group has used a variety of strategies to get good people on the FFIG bus. And most importantly, Dr. Smith has recognized that each member's role expectancy responsibility is vitally important to fulfill. In addition, his declaration that his introductory group remarks would spell out Power Boundaries was vital. In doing so, he also set structures to more nearly ensure that the most important *dys*function of a team, per Lencioni (2010), would be averted.

Lencioni (2010) describes five of what he calls Dysfunctions of a Team. In inverse order by strength of research, they are: Inattention to Results, Avoidance of Accountability, Lack of Accountability, Fear of Conflict, and Absence of Trust, with the last factor, trust, being the key issue that renders a group ineffective from both relationship and mental model perspectives. By clarifying the group's charge, Smith has ensured that the members will not be surprised when or if their recommendations are not necessarily accepted for action. The next scenario below accents similar points.

CONSENSUS IS THE ABSENCE OF LEADERSHIP—OR IS IT?

Smith was glad these questions arose. "Yes Mike, these are two very important points that are often answered too late in this kind of process. The first question is really about how the group comes to a conclusion about what actions they might take. And it's really important to address this in our opening meeting."

"So, majority rules, right? Under, let's say, Robert's Rules," said Carol.

Mike had a different point of view. "If we are trying to engage universal buy-in, then is a majority of one simply enough to be sure of that?"

Ellen agreed. "Oh no, not the dreaded consensus word, Dr. Smith."

"I'm afraid so, Ellen. Mike is right. I realize many folks aren't fond of the consensus idea."

Carol pointed out, "Ulysses would have a field day, using that card."

Dr. Smith nodded but held firm. "We want buy-in, and we want across-the-board commitment, so to use a bloc of one set of votes against another bloc's would only provoke adversarial energy, and we can't afford that. That will mean that the person or persons I appoint to facilitate the group will have to be very skilled at dialogue and understanding. They will have to work hard to develop positions so that everyone can align with the group's purpose rather than to individual agendas."

"As for your second question, I will make it clear that the group's recommendations are advisory. They can't take a position to give every student a membership in Instagram, for example. They can advise such an action, but it's our Board that has the legal authority to set policy."

Mike agreed. "Thanks for those clarifications. Absent these, we could have a runaway train on our hands. So, what is next?"

GATHERING DATA—LOTS OF IT— AND DISTILLING TO PURPOSE

John, a faculty member of the high school social studies department, and also the newest cofacilitator of the FFIG, opened the strategy session with his colleagues, Mike, Carol, Ellen, and Dr. Smith. "I think it's a good time to have a mini-debriefing session among us. We are almost done with the Information Gathering stage, and we should consider how we build from this segment to establishing purpose."

Ever the philosopher, Ellen parsed John's words. "In truth, I'm not sure we can ever say we will be through gathering information, especially about such a rapidly unfolding topic like the use of social media in teaching. This is a great example of a topic preceding the research about the very topic a group is trying to understand.

"But yes, we have done a thorough job, not only of getting good objective information, but also of taking pains to involve everyone in analyzing it."

Mike agreed. "Yes, I think we're ready to move to squeezing to purpose, with the full understanding that the purpose we establish may need to be adjusted."

Carol wasn't ready to plunge ahead yet. "I agree, but before we do, let's assess what has happened across four months of biweekly meetings."

Mike added, "Not only the biweekly meetings, but the system that you set up, Carol, in which they very actively exchanged viewpoints, opinions, additional information, and some great suggestions among themselves via the community suggestion board you set up on the school's website. That really sustained the energy."

"Thanks," Carol said. "It helped us avoid the peaks and valleys between the face-to-face meetings that really plague how these meetings typically go."

"In addition," Smith pointed out, "more than a few really great ideas emerged that might not have seen the light of day without the cyber-conversations. I really appreciate that."

She turned to the group. "So, let's debrief. What worked? Why did it work? What needs to be shored up?"

"I liked that we really took pains to provide a variety of information strategies. It's one thing to give out research articles and maybe have some presentations. It is another to build a culture of trust and effective exchange among everyone from all stakeholder corners of the school," offered John.

"The sequence building was very well planned," said Dr. Smith. "Each evening's activity was logically linked to the previous one. So, for example, Mike, when you set up guest speakers who have had social media built into their schools and followed up with the cyberwalk-through field trips of those schools, the members could view this in action on their devices at home, then process their implementation and the results they touted."

"Thanks," Mike said. "I appreciated the individual presentations Ellen put together where she brought in or showed videos about social media usage as either a plus or a minus in a school's implementation. Then, reassembling some of the speakers the next week into a panel discussion helped sharpen the issues. It was also great that we included some interested students to participate in those."

Carol laughed. "I don't know if that panel activity was a discussion or a debate, but sharpen and clarify it certainly did."

She went on. "When moderating these kinds of exchange interactions, it is important to somehow ensure that the so-called loudest voices don't dominate the thinking if others are not as articulate or are less confident in expressing their points of view publicly. Easy to talk about, difficult to control."

"Well, then, we have to count on the initial training we offered. You know, like how to drill down to root causes, and especially how to strive to understand others' thinking, like Covey (1989) offered, before being understood. Isn't that what Senge called dialogue?"

John looked at the principal. "Dr. Smith, what you did last night was an effective way to bring them around the turn."

"You mean, when he facilitated the final analysis and comparison of the issues and themes that dominated the tentative conclusions that seemed to be emerging?" said Carol. "Yes, and the Venn diagrams and charts really brought them into focus."

Mike agreed. "They are drawn out for the group to weigh against a matrix of their own thinking."

"Let's be sure we have those clear in our own minds," said Linda.

The cofacilitators' analysis demonstrates the presence of High Engagement, capacity, systems thinking, Theory U processing, and collaboration, all of which will result in decision- and action-taking. However, we can be confident of the synthesis of these variables into Futures Based Change Leadership only when the FFIG begins to formally consider futuring processes, skills, and dispositions into their analyses.

High Engagement examples are present throughout this segment. For example, Dr. Smith has not been shy to lay out power structure and consensus expectations. Dividends for his actions will thread throughout the entire process. The commentary about cyber–field trips, guest speakers, readings, and panel discussions align with the Information principle.

The Cultural Capacity to Change variables are apparent in three dimensions. Systems Disciplines appears evidenced by the group's recognition of the need for Personal Mastery to acquire the skills and dispositions necessary to consider others' viewpoints. This notion couples with Senge's Team Learning, as well.

Another capacity-to-change variable is Collaborative Leadership. When John noted the apparent congeniality among the group to participate in all the meetings and to co-contribute their thoughts, it highlights their cohesiveness.

The third dimension of cultural capacity relates to what has come to be called Design Thinking or Theory U. Other synonyms, like Creative Problem Solving, also may apply. The Theory U thinking, per Otto Scharmer (2015) in Figure 4.1 below, identifies the whole process.

Here, Scharmer's (2015) model, aptly named Theory U because he likens the process to the shape of the letter *U*, captures the whole of the

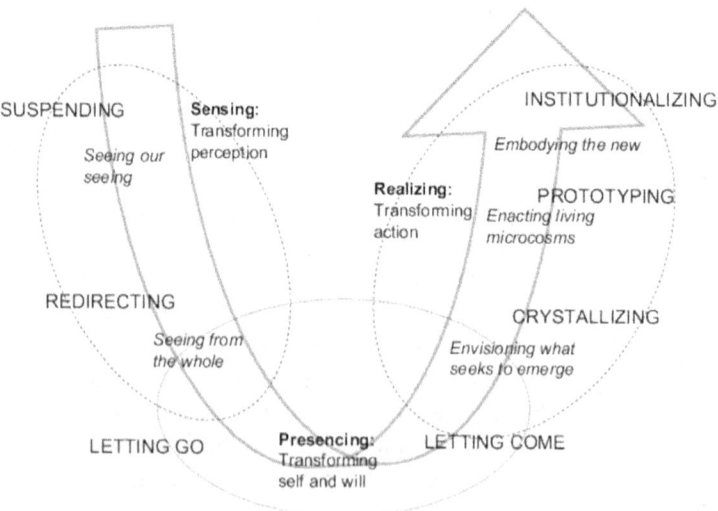

Figure 4.1.

whole change process. Starting from the upper left side of the graphic, Scharmer identifies how groups must shed old thought habits in order to transform their perception of issues and themes, and their overall mindsets in order to more nearly redirect their thinking to an ecological perception of the whole before they can create a new realization—a model to engage futures change decisioning. At this point, per the information gathering phase of Futuring I, we can see that the planning facilitators have taken great pains to prepare their members for and to expose them to a variety of information sources and to analytical exchange to enable them to come to the presencing/purpose building point that will be addressed in detail in chapter 5.

That Smith appointed not one, but four internal facilitators is interesting to consider in this preparation, information gathering, and preparation phase. Note that there are three teachers and one administrator. He apparently removed himself from the group as an active leader once he introduced the charge and the parameters. This makes sense for several reasons. The first is that a principal has many responsibilities that may dilute his ability to devote the kind of attention to the FFIG's needs. The second is that the perspectives that an apparently congenial set of individuals brings to co-planning will more nearly ensure that the FFIG will function cohesively.

Another consideration would be to bring in an outside facilitator to work with an internal facilitator to shape the team's activities and purposes. This premise has great value, especially if the issue at hand is thorny, and/or requires someone with deep expertise in channeling and provoking a group's thinking.

But now, the rubber meets the road. The group has solidified its information and must now generate their common sense of reality via agreeing on their deepest purpose.

ISSUES TO CONSIDER

To what extent has your school organization done the following?

- Provided training or specialization for team stakeholders to be versed in:
  - Collaborative Leadership Practices

- Systems' Disciplines
- Design Thinking/Theory U dispositions
- Futures forecasting dimensions and skills
- Used an outside facilitator/consultant to collaborate with an internal facilitator to take the group through the entire futuring process

ESSENTIAL POINTS

1. Decisions are only as good as the extent to which stakeholders both have all the information they need and the ability to parse it. Participants can expect as many as five phases of work to complete their tasks:
   - Phase I: Information Gathering/Purpose Building
   - Phase II: If-Then Two-Dimensional Futuring
   - Phase III: Three-Dimensional Futuring Scenario Development
   - Phase IV: Adapt or Transform?
   - Phase V: Action Design

2. This phase, Phase I, includes two tasks:
   - Information Gathering
   - Purpose Building

3. Information Gathering relies on the creativity of the process planners to include:
   - A cross-section of presenters
   - A cross-section representation of viewpoints
   - Assurances that participants can objectively distill data in order to build conclusions that will drive purpose construction

4. Purpose Building relies heavily on Theory U thinking, where participants must shed old thinking habits for new ways to realize in order to drill down to deepest purpose(s).
   - This is a tender pivot point in the process that requires deft facilitation.

5. Phase I is the foundation for all that follows.

Chapter Five

Processing to Purpose

Organic over Inorganic Every Time

"I'm going to offer my favorite quote," Dr. Smith said. He cleared his throat and recited, *"We did not put our ideas together. We put our purposes together... And we agreed"* (Senge et al., *Presencing*, 2004). "That's what we saw when the FFIG began to drill down to purpose," he concluded.

Ever the wordsmith, Ellen spoke up. "Boss, is the verb 'drill' what we experienced?"

Mike offered, "I like when we debrief like this by examining our language usage. And I agree that the word 'drill' suggests a kind of regimented process that our member colleagues may have used to get from point X to point Y. But, in fact, it surely didn't unfold like that at all."

"I'm not sure what you mean," said John. "They did get down to what I thought was a deep purpose that arose out of considerable dialogue and processing."

"Yes," agreed Ellen, "but if we had a video recording, we'd see that their journey was far from an agenda-driven, step-by-step, logical evolution. And that's fine. It was pleasing to see how the committee had the group maturity to bounce from idea and theme to include a variety of points and views and then organically unite around their purpose."

"That's my point," said Dr. Smith. "That quote is profound. It's an old Mayan proverb, by the way, and it captures how a deep purpose only arises when ideas and 'I-thinks' are burned off and a group coalesces around synthesizing their truest intents. That they did, after yes, a not-so-neat process of exchanges and clarifications, and a lot of active listening."

Carol added, "Yes, and I'm glad we brought in an outside facilitator to help the group work that through. We cofacilitators have good skills, but Dr. Richards was clearly very much an expert at helping the members navigate the purpose maze."

"So, let's do some backward engineering on what their purpose has captured," suggested Mike.

Group evolution, for its collective and connected effectiveness, is more nearly an example of a jazz ensemble's session rather than of a formal orchestra concert. Whilst jazz musicians are playing on the fly, it is not so easy to discern how the creation of musical energies they synthesize comes to pass. However, afterward it seems far easier to parse the music for its notes and rhythms. In short, the facilitators have rightly recognized that a given cookbook strategy to elicit a group buy-in of their collective purpose is not likely to work.

This organic rather than inorganic process must be recognized. Moreover, the process is better led by an individual who has experience in role expectancy, group maintenance activities, and intragroup communication skills. Where it may sometimes seem economical to avoid the expense of an outside facilitator to help move a group through a complicated process, having an experienced and skilled one can save time, minimize confusion, more nearly ensure the kind of common understanding a successful, cohesive group requires.

Here, the distinction between pasted compromise and an organic, natural coalition of thinking and dispositions is noteworthy where the latter is far more desirable as the prescient Mayan quote affirms. If the "paste" of a "pact" weakens, so, too, does the purpose, so, too, does the commitment to the purpose they cobbled together. If the purpose breaks down, futuring becomes scattershot at best.

Carol read back the purpose. *"The ABC FFIG recognizes that our school is committed to its obligation to continuously upgrade the capacity of its teaching and learning by using social media to promote interactivity and critical thinking as our prime academic goal. At the same time, this committee recognizes and is committed to practicing safe and positive practices of social media among its stakeholders."*

John smiled. "Not bad. We have Dr. Richards to thank for his skills. But the group members certainly deserve recognition."

"Who was as surprised as I was when Ulysses, the union president, in essence broke the deadlock between those who were avoiding the premise that social media was a tool to upgrade the overall instructional skills of our professional staff, and those who rejected out of hand, first of all, that social media had any place in teaching and learning, let alone for communication purposes?" asked Mike.

Carol offered, "I understand the naysayers' resistance. A lot of negative news comes out of the distorted uses of social media, not only in schools but across the board. Mike, you've already spoken to that, and by the way, you were very eloquent when you described how misuse of social media has impacted our students often very adversely."

"Thanks," said Mike. "Yes, there were some very sad and disturbing occurrences that troubled me to recount with the group. I was reluctant to dredge up those very memories. The other was that those with a confirmation bias against social media would seize the data I was presenting to use it to advance their opposition."

John asked, "Confirmation bias?"

"Yes," said Mike. "It's a premise that people will cherry-pick any evidence to strengthen their own biased beliefs without objectively considering all the information they might need in order to reach an objective conclusion."

Smith nodded. "We are all guilty of that, I suppose. I know I am sometimes. And I agree with Carol that having Dr. Richards point out that pitfall seemed to heighten everyone's wariness of falling into that trap."

"And when it did happen—for example, when Mrs. Jones, the PTA president, seized on Mike's presentation to rally her anti–social media supporters—it was great that Dr. Richards allowed someone else to ask her if Mrs. Jones's reaction was an example of confirmation bias."

"Well, she didn't answer directly. He left it to the group to mull over and express their insights. A nice example of constructivist empowerment," offered Carol.

"In the end, the group really seemed to evolve," said Ellen.

"Maybe the most difficult part of this phase was making sense of the phase's expectations," said John. "Yes, it was an information and distilling phase. Indeed, each of the phases are evolutions of distilling and creating. Yet it was also intended to get to a coalesced purpose. There were a lot of moving parts."

"Yes," agreed Dr. Smith. "You all arranged for a variety of activities to enable the group to see the information sets from different angles. I have to say that the panel discussion–slash–debate crystallized the issues at stake very well for me."

"I liked the cyber field trips you set up, Ellen. That must have been difficult to put together," said Mike.

"Well, I had to be very careful to be objective. I had to rely on research in various journals and books to find sources that would engage the subgroups I created to review the material and squeeze it down to their basic essences. The review guides we gave them were helpful. On top of that, there were some computer competencies that I had to backfill. One was that some members had difficulty accessing the information online. Another was that if they were able to directly communicate online with the authors and experts we offered, they needed to craft their questions for them carefully."

"Was it difficult for the subgroups to communicate with each other, too?" asked John.

"That was a hurdle for some, but they overcame it," said Ellen. "However, this part of the process, not only for this phase but for the ones to follow, was really important. Ongoing conversation *in between* public face-to-face meetings kept the engagement momentum much more continuous than the more traditional kind of committee work we are all used to."

"Yes," agreed Carol. "It was helpful that each of us took a subgroup to facilitate. Necessary, actually, because while this group will eventually be our think tank, their skills still need to be developed."

Mike offered, "What may have been most powerful was the focus group interviews we did. It was great to have representative samples of parents, teachers, and students, first in separate groups and then comingled, to try to tease out their own themes and patterns."

Smith used this comment to make an important point. "It seemed it was the teachers who drove down to the deepest issue."

"Well, yes, you're right, but not until our instructional leaders, especially the content chairs, pointed out that the students' academic performances were wanting from a number of yardstick standpoints," said John. "That was a tough pill to swallow for the teachers to hear."

"Yes," said Ellen. "It was. And I appreciate their sensitivity. Of course, they want their students to do well. I was happy that Ulysses, the union president, didn't throw a tantrum. Instead he invited a conversation about why academics were inadequate. And then Dr. Richards blunted the blame throwing by inviting some creative thinking."

"Yes, 'creative thinking'—all too often the weak sister of groups' skill sets," said Dr. Smith. "I need to work on that myself as I work with the staff on various issues."

Carol sounded defensive. "Dr. Smith, I'm glad you acknowledged that we all need to work on that, and you do know that creative problem solving wasn't even in our vocabulary, let alone part of our culture, until very recently."

Smith recognized Carol's reaction. "Yes, I do know that. We all need to realize that we can't snap our fingers and create creativity. We have begun to practice some creativity techniques, and I am glad that Dr. Richards used some strategies at that juncture to enable the group to reframe the academic deficit issues' dissatisfaction away from the blame game, toward realizing that everyone will benefit from being open to using new processes, methodologies, and techniques to reach our students."

"And thus, the crowning point," John offered, "when the group recognized how social media, properly used, can promote and sustain a new kind of interactive, high-engagement kind of learning culture!"

Smith smiled. "I didn't script that, but I couldn't have been happier to see how the group's purposes seemed to mesh together after that segment."

There is much to glean and to model when considering this scenario. Think about the complexities of group and task process that have been analyzed about the following:

- Group comfort and trust to exchange;
- An absence of a fear of conflict;
- The ability to synthesize purposes, deep purposes;
- Recognizing confirmation bias;
- Constructivist empowerment;
- Planning interactive activities;
- Ensuring that group members master knowledge high engagement strategies;

- Using creative problem-solving processes that depend on divergent thinking, and its welding with convergent thinking; and
- Coalescing purpose deeper than originally charged.

These can be roughly divided into two categories within the subsets of the Knowledge Component of the High Engagement Model discussed in chapter 2. Recall that the Knowledge Component consisted of mastery and application of specific school organization skills necessary for effective decision making. It also consisted of the more subtle, but equally powerful dimension of human relationships.

The developments in this phase corresponding with *Organizational Knowledge and Skills* would be:

- Constructivist empowerment;
- Planning interactive activities;
- Ensuring that group members master knowledge High Involvement Model strategies; and
- Using creative problem-solving processes that depend on divergent thinking, and its welding with convergent thinking.

The developments most nearly correlated with the *Human Relations* necessity within the Knowledge component would be:

- Group comfort and trust to exchange;
- An absence of a fear of conflict;
- The ability to synthesize purposes, deep purposes; and
- Recognizing confirmation bias.

Constructivist empowerment refers to the process expectation that recognizes how the participants' immersion in the experiential soup of data and exchange begin to self-develop, sometimes with guidance from individuals like a Dr. Richards–like facilitator, that is, someone who self-constructs his own knowledge schema. These models then become probed for truth by others to eventually coalesce to an evolved sense.

Planning interactive activities highlights how the group facilitators took great pains to educate the participants and to provide catalytic interaction and process exchange per the constructivist empowerment theme described above. The facilitators had provided for presentations, panels, debates, field trips, cyber field trips and interviews, and focus group analyses. Importantly, and again as before, per the constructivist empowerment notion, the facilitators had prepared guides and questions to help the participants parse the data they needed to consider. We can assume that the facilitators also made room for both cyber-exchange as well as face-to-face interaction in the live meetings.

Ensuring that group members master Knowledge High Engagement Model strategies prioritizes the idea that a group does not become effective by luck very often. Rather, embedding these variables requires conscious planning for effective presence. Thus, as already pointed out above, the Knowledge variable particularly is accounted for.

Using creative problem-solving processes that depend on divergent thinking, and its welding with convergent thinking, is a highlight issue. How can a group innovate if the culture has not made room for it to innovate? How can a culture be creative if the creativity variables of fluency, flexibility, elaboration, and originality are not nurtured? In this scenario, we see that Dr. Richards takes pains to use creativity skills so that the group will recognize their value in the deliberation and use them in creating an alchemy of new perspectives and ideas.

In complementary balance are the themes associated with relationships processes that drive the evolution of an effective group. The conversation about the FFIG's interactions and the recognition of these collaborations reveal much about the FFIG's potential effectiveness and serve as good guideposts to consider in any futuring process.

Group comfort and trust to exchange was particularly noticeable and representative of Lencioni's description of the presence of trust in any group as the most foundational factor to ensure. This was evident when the union president felt free to voice his differing opinions and Mrs. Jones's opposition to the use of social media had their chances to be heard and recognized with respect.

An absence of a fear of conflict was also cited by Lencioni as an important behavior to look for. By the same token, linked with the factor noted above (group trust) is the fact that while the group seemed to have voiced various objections and yes-buts, the group also recognized that healthy, respectful conflict had its place in the sun. Were the group filled with mutual yes-men, it is assured that the quality of their eventual dialogue would have been superficial.

The ability to synthesize deep purposes could not have happened without extensive dialogue per Senge's Team Learning Discipline principle (*Schools That Learn* 2016) and the active listening skills that enabled the groups to presence, as Otto Scharmer terms it, its deepest intentions (*Presence* 2004). Presencing can be considered a synonym for the end product of shedding old ways of thinking, the use of active listening skills, and deep thinking, to arrive at the "place" where the collective realization emerges. This presencing phenomenon is dependent on nurturing via a variety of processes and strategies.

Recognizing confirmation bias (Kahneman, 2011) highlights a group logic process that is representative of a body of analytical skills necessary to arrive at the "truth." This point may actually belong in both categories of the High Engagement Model. On the one hand, the recognition of ILL-logical archetypes, like confirmation bias, is an organizational process associated with effective decision making. However, on the other hand, the conversation in the scenario more nearly depicted the situation from a group process, human relations perspective. When Mrs. Jones "committed" the act of confirmation bias, Dr. Richards let the group recognize her line of so-called logic, was rewarded with *their* recognition of confirmation bias, and saw how Mrs. Jones self-corrected for it.

Returning to the Tower of Babel notion, where we attribute the gods' deterring of a successful construct by humans, we see additional possible variables at play when a group aspires to construct common meaning from a hodgepodge of data, communication, and viewpoint definitions. In essence, as Raellin (2016) notes, an effective group must engage many themes, acculturate many practices, and master many principles to establish, as he calls it, a common sense of reality.

This complexity emphasizes the importance of group training, preparation, and evolution so that the group is able to circle its wagons around the true purposes they seek to presence.

The stage now appears set to use the increased capacity of the organizational culture, especially in terms of its Systems Disciplines mastery, practices in Theory U processes and creative thinking, and the use of Collaborative Leadership principles to begin exploring two dimensional forecasting skills and dispositions in order to identify the most probable futures they will need to parse in order to meet their purpose.

ISSUES TO CONSIDER

To what extent does your school organization do the following:

- Have the skills dimensions of Collaborative Leadership, Theory U/ Design Thinking creativity, and intragroup "maturity" to engage deep purpose building?
- Have the ability to discern data's implications from varieties of Information Gathering sources?
- Internally accept the Mayan proverb we cited earlier?

ESSENTIAL POINTS

1. A "cookbook" process to evolve a group's effectiveness may capture what happened, but it rarely characterizes the sequence in which the effectiveness evolves. However:
   - The guideposts it provides enables the facilitator(s) to recognize the process.
   - Futuring processes depend on deep purpose generation as the essential foundation, which has evolved from smart information gathering and analysis.
2. Per Lencioni, a group that does not permit objections and differences to prevailing opinions will be dysfunctional.
3. Confirmation bias is a premise where people will cherry-pick any evidence to strengthen their own inclined beliefs without objectively considering all the information they might need in order to reach an objective conclusion.
4. Effective Information Gathering planning requires a spectrum of approaches and provisions for objective inquiry.
5. In addition, multiple strategies for communication are necessary.

Chapter Six

Futuring II
Future Wheeling the Future

Dr. Richards looked over the FFIG. He knew he was going to have fun because the group had quickly coalesced to purpose, had shed old habits of thinking, and was ready to begin a process that was about to engage them in formal futuring processes.

He knew that these futuring processes, indeed, were both new and old to them. That is, on the one hand, all people *future*, as in "plan," "prepare for," "anticipate," "dread," "look forward to," "avoid," etc., in virtually all of their conscious and sometimes not-so-conscious decision making. Indeed, a case could be made for other living creatures' *futuring*, too. Squirrels bury acorns; birds build nests; trees shed leaves.

On *this* hand, however, he was bridging from their so-called natural futuring processes over to more formal and multidimensional thinking that would require both a mastery of skills and, more importantly, a dispositional change that would hopefully transform them both as individuals and as a whole, so they would be able to foresee possibilities, probabilities, and preferabilities they might never have thought were within their capacity.

He meant to have them master two-dimensional thinking; three-dimensional forecasting; scenario building; adaptive or transformative decisioning; and deep, intentional action design—all grounded in serving the coalesced purpose they had evolved about the role action design might play in their school's instructfigional energies insofar as this applied to social media policy.

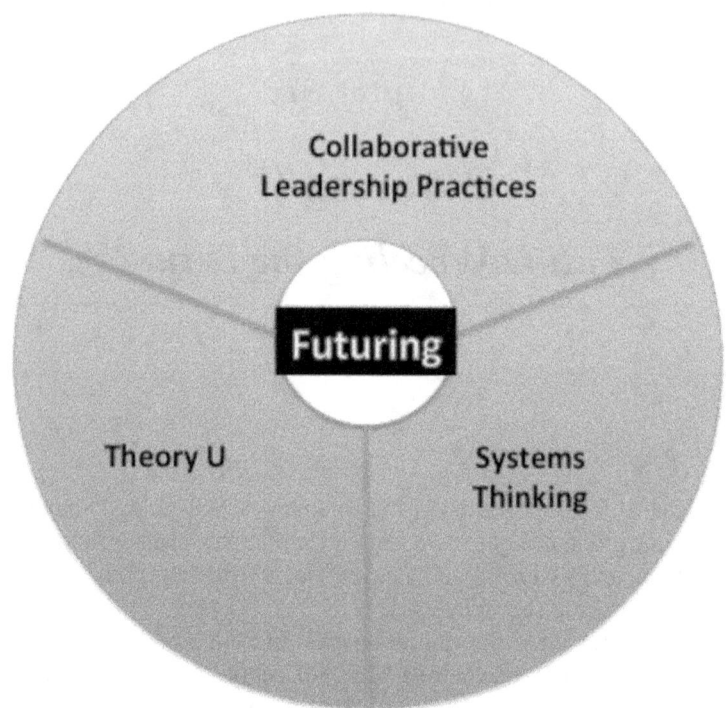

Figure 6.1.

The sum of his work with them, he knew, would actively engage them in an intersection of behaviors, skills, and strategies to solidify this cultural capacity to change. These included decision making, cultural analysis, and alignment with purpose building; Theory U–design thinking processes; and attention to Senge's learning organization disciplines; in addition to futuring.

It was important for him to remind himself, and likely his clients, that these needs would be addressed organically, rather than its opposite. That is, priority activities and experiences would emerge among the interactivity of the group. He, as facilitator, would have to be an on-his-feet diagnostician, able to slide in and out of discussions and actions on the fly to stay ahead of their direction and to sail with their intentions as appropriate.

"I'm tired!" declared Dr. Richards. "There was lot of energy in the group today."

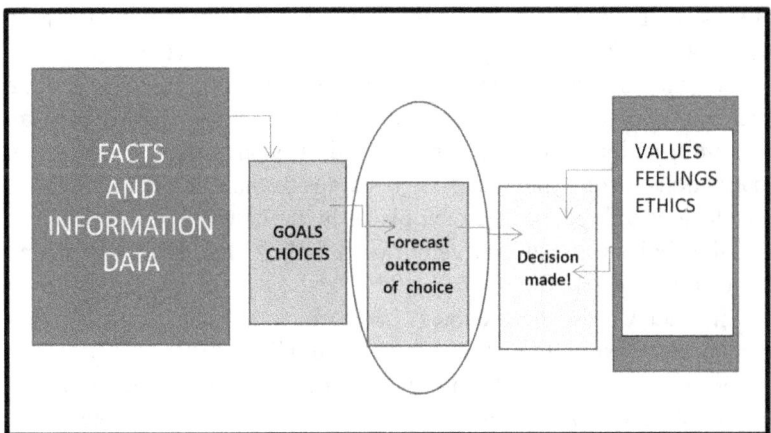

Figure 6.2.

Principal Smith agreed. "I'm tired, too, just from watching."

"I certainly don't diminish what you and your colleagues contributed. You were all terrific," said Richards.

"I liked how you began with that decision model," said Mike. "It brought attention to how recognizing even this simple, linear frame was a basis for understanding the processes they were undertaking."

"Well, even though the model is simple, it certainly highlighted how they needed to weld the data that had led them to this undertaking. The concern, both about how social media usage in the school was pervading our students' personal lives and its potential capacity to both influence their learning and our instructional attentions, was critical," said Carol.

Smith agreed. "Yes, it was necessary to draw continued awareness to that. And since, as we have agreed many times, per Scharmer, energy *does* follow attention, that enabled us to reaffirm the overarching goal we had generated."

"Once I was sure that the twig was bent, I felt the need to have them recognize the potential choices before them," offered Dr. Richards.

"Except you didn't use the term 'choices'; instead, you introduced them as alternative futures, possible futures," said Ellen. "Each choice considered suggested a thread-direction that might spin effects that require an evolution of their thinking."

"I think I will be the futuring Grinch here for a moment," said John. "It's important to realize that they only generated four choices, or alternative futures, as you call them. We need to recognize that these may not have been the *only* choices they could have made."

"A very important point, John," said Richards. "That was why the segment that preceded where we took them today was so critical. The information gathering, the panel discussions, the exchanges and interactions among them, and the reactions to their points of view and conclusions offered, needed their places in the ABC High School sun so that the choices agreed to were not willy-nilly, 'The Martians will land tomorrow' possible futures."

"In other words, these choices had to have substantial justification behind them," said Ellen. "And that they did."

Richards agreed. "And what will happen as they plunge more formally into the process? In fact, you saw it today—these choices will twist, turn, and morph, sometimes when we least expect it."

"What will you do then, Dr. Richards?" asked the principal.

"Oh, I will let new ideas evolve anywhere they emerge," said Richards. "To smother them would negate the creative problem-solving skills we must also nurture along the way. However, I would allow dialogue, but not conversation—the difference being that the former promotes the kind of exchange muscles we need to keep the whole in futures-based mode. And the latter is just a hodgepodge of 'I-thinks'."

"Thanks for the clarification," John said.

"Hmm, seems like you're developing us, too," said Ellen.

Richards smiled. "You were developing before I arrived, but the answer is yes, of course I am. If you are to sustain the actions that will emerge from this very ambitious process and be able to embed this process into other futuring needs, it is this group that will have the necessary capacity to continue the journey after I ride out of town."

"Let's talk about the Futures Wheels generation," said Carol. "It was interesting to see the group engage the process, I think because it is such a natural if-then progression."

The conversation described above describes and reaffirms, of necessity, a synthesis of the themes and principles explored in chapter 5, with the transition to the two-dimensional, if-then futuring strategies of chapter 6. Dr. Richards, the outside facilitator, and the internal planning group we have already met observed some key pivot points that will successfully lead the group through the initial Futuring II. These were:

- The premise of futuring is not a new one. However, where we use futuring in this book, it refers to the *organizational* need to learn the skills, competencies, and dispositions of futuring as an acculturated part of its practices.
- The premises of Possible, Probable (or Emerging), and Preferable futures are key to this mindset.
- The organizational challenge is to eventually determine how, after much deliberation, creativity, and dialogue, the group think tank can recognize to what extent the probable emerging future they project aligns with their preferable future.
- This would lead to three other phases: *Three-Dimensional/Scenario-Generating Futuring, Adapt or Transform Conclusions, and Action Designing with Coalesced Purpose.*
- Energy follows attention.
- Decisioning is a product of aligning values with projected futuring strategies, with deep goal setting.
- Building futuring capacity deserves priority focus.

Union president Ulysses looked at the Futures Wheel. He asked, "How do we do this? How do we use a futures wheel to forecast the future?"

Dr. Richards answered, "Not one specific future, Ulysses. This device will help us identify the Possible, the Probable, and the Preferable futures, especially the Probable ones."

Ulysses asked, "How?"

"What you do is put the idea, the theme, the Emerging Future at hand, in the center circle. Then you ripple effect from that."

Now Ulysses got it. "Okay, I see it now. It forces us to realize there are multiple futures before us that can be at least somewhat calculated."

Richards smiled. "There's more, but that is how you use a Futures Wheels to make a model of Possible, Probable, and Preferable Futures."

Dr. Smith exclaimed, "Very well. Let's start thinking this way!"

Richards continued, "For example, we put 'continuing brain drain for young adults' in the center. What would be a natural effect of that future?"

Dr. Smith offered, "Property values might drop."

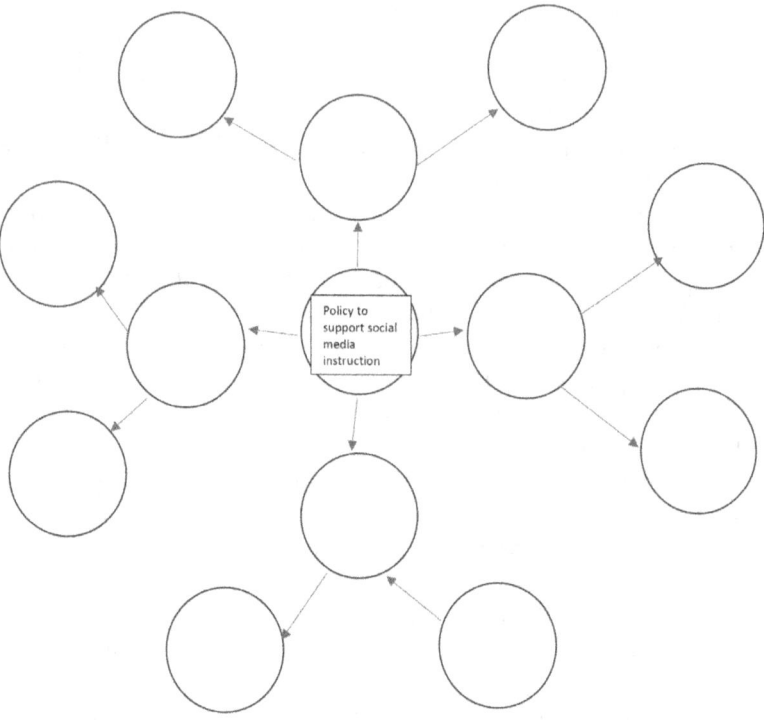

Figure 6.3.

"Okay," Dr. Richards responded. He wrote that into a circle that branched off from the center future. "And what might *that* future breed?"

PTA president Pat answered, "Well, that might make moving to ABC more affordable for additional minority, underfinanced populations."

Student council president Samantha shot her hand up. "That would tie in with what the demographer guest speaker suggested."

Richards agreed. "Great point, and if we extend that future thread, we can see outcomes of outcomes."

Barry, a member of the business community, spoke up. "My subgroup came up with one that we thought tied in with the economic themes we discussed a few weeks back. The economic and social health of the ABC community is connected with the ability of our ABC High School, indeed the entire district system, to reflect the highest possible values and school capacity to create students able to contribute to the community's viability. If we are not able to help our school staff to transform its instruction, we will not be able to sustain either the school or the community that it serves. So, an alternative future might very well be that our industrial and commercial bases would be interested in fostering effective internships for our students."

Richards smiled. "Do we see that this might be a likely probable future?" When no one objected, he said, "All right, let's agree that it is."

"I'm going to be the futures Grinch again," said John. After the group affably groaned, he went on, "We can't forget that our FFIG has turned its attention, and therefore its energy, to the use of social media in how we deliver world-class instruction to our students. But that wasn't how it started."

"Yes, John is right. We turned that way for sure, and rightfully so," offered social studies teacher Al. "Originally we had, and we still have, major and legitimate concerns about the negative impact that students' use of social media has had on their emotional health and their feelings of well-being, not to mention discipline issues."

Pupil personnel director Arthurs agreed. "So, to take another prospective alternative future, a possible-probable future is that we *ignore* the issue of students' use of social media. And imagine where that futures thread takes us."

This brought several responses, all objecting to this notion, and they prompted Dr. Richards to caution the participants. "Ms. Arthurs is chiding your thinking. Like it or not, she offers a Possible future here, and perhaps a Probable one, too. That you object so strongly to the idea implies that you are leapfrogging to a *probable* future that you do *not* prefer! I have to remind you that we are not ready to solidify preferables or nonpreferables at this stage."

Principal Smith offered a different perspective. "So, Dr. Richards, and my meeting colleagues, would you agree that an alternative future to add to the wheel would be that the district explored model policies about student usage of social media?"

Richards was satisfied with the FFIG progress in constructing a futures wheel. He was pleased that the preceding Information phase had led them to offer possible futures that were viable within the context of the data and analyses they had invested into the process. And he saw the opportunity to leverage their thinking to the next necessity of this If-Then, Phase Two activity phase.

They were ready to further their futuring by agreeing to what they thought were the Probable Futures they would need to chart to move to Phase Three, Three-Dimensional Futuring.

They were ready to parse to Probable Futures.

"We are ready to do some serious futuring now," he explained to the leadership team.

"How so?" asked Mike. "They've been really terrific already"

"Oh yes!" agreed Dr. Richards. "For sure. Now we have formalized the thinking I had to delay earlier."

"You mean the Preferable Futures they began to offer?" asked John.

"We can't really stifle that. Shouldn't, in fact. Preferable futuring is certainly a natural part of their journey. But like a flower, we can't force it to bloom before it is ready to flourish. And frankly, they need to begin to more clearly define the Probable Futures that are hidden among the possible futures they have considered."

Ellen asked, "How will we do that?"

"It will be straightforward, and I will need your help." said Dr. Richards. "We will divide the team into five groups, one for each of you to facilitate. Using the futures wheel we will display, ask your members to agree on one or two, even three Probable futures.

"A Probable future," he went on, "is one that can be reasonably accepted by the team because the data analyses substantiate the future they have identified."

"Then we offer them to the whole group for more discussion?" asked Dr. Smith.

"Not exactly. After they establish consensus about several Probable Futures, again with the proviso that we are not necessarily pinpointing Preferable Futures, I will introduce a new futuring technique before we move to the next phase. That phase, Three-Dimensional Futuring, will depend mightily on the quality of these exchanges. The next technique is called Cross-Impact Thinking and is a natural beneficiary of the quality of their future wheeling."

The puzzle pieces that have come together begin to indicate their whole. We can now see how a coalescence of processes and purpose has moved the fledgling think-tank futurist group along an inorganic and organic continuum toward creating their preferable future. This began with sorting through, exchanging, distilling, and drawing tentative conclusions about the issues, trends, events, and dispositions. Their consideration of the probable cross currents' intersections has helped them begin to get their arms around their Emerging/Probable Future. They begin to see how these relate to their high school's need to get its arms around the elephant that is social media's influence in their school.

As they began to shave down to a clearer purpose, they realized that they needed to understand how the school's embedding social media's capacity into its instructional arsenal would transform learning. And in addition, they continue to recognize that a policy for how the school responds to emotional and disciplinary issues is connected to social media's use by the students and the community.

ISSUES TO CONSIDER

To what extent does your school organization:

- Relate the premise of futuring to its purpose?
- Connect its collective disposition about the very premise of futuring to its culture's basic beliefs?
- Relate the points distilled from the Information Gathering–Purpose Building Phase to support its possible, probable, and preferred futures?

ESSENTIAL POINTS

1. The concept of "futuring" seems foreign at first, yet its premise is built into how we exist.
2. Yet the concept of futuring in school systems is often given short shrift in favor of quick, superficial thinking.
3. Decision making and futuring are codependent.
4. There are many futures forecasting strategies a school think tank can put to effective use and that should become part of the school's culture.
5. There are three kinds of futures: possible, probable, and preferable.

6. Two-dimensional forecasting techniques, like trend extrapolation, futures wheels, and cross impact matrices, effectively enable a think tank to narrow to reasoned probable futures.

Chapter Seven

Futuring II Continued
Cross Impact Futuring

Samantha, the student council president, looked at the union president, Ulysses. "Mr. Joyce, it's so strange that I feel that we can talk about our work on this committee. I mean, after all, you've been my Advanced Placement teacher for two years. And now we are sort of equals."

Ulysses smiled. "Not 'sort of,' Samantha. On this committee we are equals, and I daresay that your input has more value than mine. After all, you represent the entire student body, and their experience and perspectives are vital."

Samantha appreciated that. "Well, we're both presidents. And the process we are developing needs multiple points of view."

"For sure," Ulysses said. "And while it took me a bit to figure out how to do a futures wheel to project possible, probable, and preferable futures—"

"You mean the 'Three Ps,' Mr. Joyce, for short." Samantha smiled.

"Yes, the 'Three Ps.' I can see, though, that the futures wheels thinking was a stepping-stone to this process, the Cross-Impact Matrix."

"I think I understand it, said Samantha. "It reminds me of a skill we learned in Mrs. Chris's Creative Writing class. That was called 'force fitting.' What we do is list the most probable futures we think that the futures wheels evolved along the y-axis."

Ulysses held up his hand. "I am an English teacher, Ms. Fonerina. I wouldn't know what a y-axis was unless it looked like Winston Churchill."

Samantha searched for a simple metaphor. "Mr. Joyce, think of the y-axis as a longitudinal line, you know, running north and south."
The light went on for Mr. Joyce, "Okay, then, the x-axis is the latitudinal line?"
"Yes," she said. "And now you can see we have a grid."
"Very well. So we write one probable future, an alternative future, we have agreed is supported by our information gathering phase and our small group analyses in the boxes along the left side of the chart, I mean the matrix."
"Then we 'force fit'."
Ulysses shook his head. "'Force fit'?"
"You take different ideas or issues and project what might happen if somehow they were merged," Samantha offered. "For example, if we merged a bracelet with a phone, we'd have an..."
"Apple Watch!" Ulysses smiled. "And if we considered how, for example, a strategy to embed social media into teachers' instructional practices and see how this might impact with teachers . . . Well, we'd have to really dip back into our discussions in the Information-Gathering Stages, but I recall teachers were wary of the idea but open to it with the proper support."

Table 7.1.

Goal: Identify practices where social media may be used in instruction	Teachers	Students	Community
Strategy 1: Form a committee to review exemplary practices in other schools.	• Could be wary of the committee's intent • Would want more information	• Could be eager to contribute • Might object if they don't have devices to use social media	• Would demand parameters • Would want guidance on how students might benefit
Strategy 2.??	??	??	??

Samantha smiled. "By George—or by Mr. Joyce—I think we've got it."

"By Ulysses, Ms. Samantha."

Another group was having a vigorous conversation, too. They were Pete Politician, Charles Chairman, Constance Community, and Patricia Parent. Principal Smith had specifically invited these individuals to be committee members for several reasons. The first was that they had expressed deep interest in the issues to be studied. He also thought their perspectives and specialties would help the Whole determine the most likely emerging, probable futures. Smith had advocated for them even more specifically for their expertise areas: Peter Politician was deeply committed to the improvement of the ABC High School. He saw the school as the cornerstone for the community, and he rightly realized that its success would have much to do with maintaining the community's overall health. However, and more importantly, his skills of collaborative leadership were recognized by everyone. And Smith thought that would be a valuable factor as the futuring process deepened.

Charles Chairman, the head of the school's small but lively philosophy department, also had two strengths that would aid the committee. One was his deep popularity with students of all types in the high school. As comfortable with student athletes as he was with scholars, he also had a great rapport with students who traveled on the fringes of the school active networks, as well. But in addition, his interest in creative thinking and his ability to teach it was well-known and respected. Smith and Facilitator Richards were equally hopeful he could add that process skill to the committee's deliberative flow.

Constance Community was a well-known figure in the area, as a businessperson for one, where she ran one of the few remaining successful stores in the town. Her interest in local economic issues, as well as in understanding the community's evolving demographic trends, also made her an active voice in any meaningful plans the group might conjure. These skills made her a kind of futurist.

Patricia Parent's role and participation was clearly essential, and her reputation as a vocal opponent of students' use of social media, both in and out of school, while potentially an obstructionist behavior, deserved its place in the dialogue, and in this case, in the convergent and divergent thinking that would take turns dominating the conversation in

58   Chapter Seven

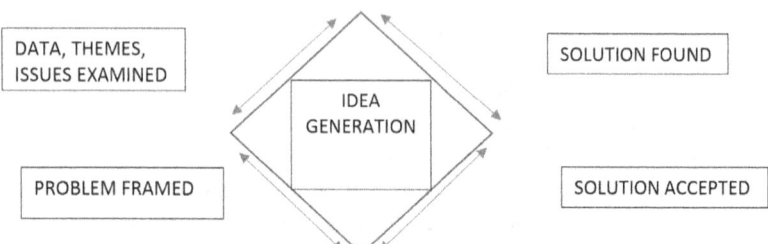

Figure 7.1.

order to construct a valid Cross Impact Matrix. This emphasis would also help her keep the systems issues before the group.

In fact, Dr. Richards had repeatedly made points about the differences between convergent and divergent thinking: He'd shown a diagram:

One session went something like this. He pointed to the diagram of creative problem solving. He said, "I want you to look at this simple diagram, but before I explain it or rather, have you figure it out, who can tell me the first thought that comes to mind when I say 'ship'?"

The group looked around, and Anthony, the head custodian, said, "The *Santa Maria.*"

Richards said nothing and continued to wait for other responses.

Susan, the science teacher, said, "Okay, the *Nina.*"

More silence from Richards. Additional answers stayed on the same thread, for example, the *Titanic* and the USS *Constitution*. Then someone said, "How about the *Starship Enterprise?*"

The group smiled, realizing they had extended their thinking, and Richards confirmed that. Yet he persisted by waiting for more answers.

The wait time became heavy. Finally, Richards said, "What about Friend*ship*? Citizen*ship*? Or, for that matter, one-upman*ship*?"

Peter Politician groaned. "Now you've got a whole different highway we could have traveled!"

"And the message behind my music?" Richards asked.

More silence, then Rosemary Rotary offered, "We were so locked in on our first internal visual of the word 'ship' that we blocked out the possibility of considering different angles."

"And in doing that, we were..." said Chuck.

"In doing that," said Richards, "you were using only your linear thinking instead of the three-dimensional thinking we will need to meet the group's purpose."

He continued, "At the risk of upsetting some of you, have you ever thought that it is possible that a scientist could already be looking at the cure for cancer through a microscope? However, her energy is so focused on one result that she overlooks the other, perhaps more promising premise the data may provide? In this committee, and particularly as we cross over from Phase II, If-Then Thinking, to deeper futuring, it is important that we navigate between convergent and divergent thinking modes and, quite frankly, spend the bulk of our time at this point, on the latter."

"Convergent and divergent?" asked Rosemary.

He pointed to the diagram. "It's pretty simple, deceptively simple," he said. "Columbus sailed the ocean blue in?" He didn't wait for them to answer. "Two plus two is?" Again, he didn't wait. "These are examples of *con*vergent thinking."

"Now, my question about ships is not a convergent thinking one at first glance. Here is another example: 'Name all the uses for a spoon.' Here's another: 'Who actually discovered America?' 'What criteria should I consider in voting for a candidate?'"

"Okay," said Ellen. "So *con*vergent thinking is typically one single-point, 'correct' answer. But *di*vergent thinking requires that we think in multiples, creatively?"

The group nodded. But Mike, the resident Grinch, needed clarification. "All good, Dr. Richards, we appreciate the distinction and recognize your expectation. But for sure, there are times when the group will need to *con*verge, too?"

"So glad you said that, Mike," replied Dr. Richards. "You are correct, and that is why this diagram is so important to understand. Take a look, and 'read' it from left to right. On the left side, you will see terms like 'data finding.' You will also see, on the right side, terms like 'problem solution' and 'problem acceptance.' Notice the lines and arrows that describe the diamond shape between these *con*vergent expectations. You can see the arrows that point *to* these terms are meant to imply *con*vergence."

"Ah," said Mike, "*but* the arrows then widen out and capture the term 'idea generation' within the diamond before they converge on the right side again. I am taking that to mean that is when we are expected to think *di*vergently, otherwise known as 'creatively'."

"Exactly," said Richards. "That segment is where I will introduce several creativity techniques that extend beyond your current understanding of creative thinking. And most importantly, that is where I would like you to keep your mindset as you consider how the probable futures you've presently narrowed to may be affected by or may affect the issues, themes, groups, or individuals in the matrix, along the x-axis."

"Hmm, I am getting the idea that the matrix boxes not only can have different mini-futures within them, but that they can also vary from group to group, especially as we begin to converge away from diverge," said Carol.

"Let's see how that plays out," Richards replied. After a segment in which mini-groups processed the Cross-Impact Matrix, he called a halt and remarked, "Pete Politician, Charles Chairman, Constance Community, and Patricia Parent's group turned out to be the textbook example of how a group might parse probable and possible impacts on given factors."

Patricia Parent reflected, "Well, we had a common purpose as the rest of the member groups did, but the way it broke, each person had a perspective that was different from the other and played that role in the discussion. I think maybe I was trying to point out the systems disciplines issues that we had to consider."

Constance Community broke in. "True enough, Pat. I also think we were playing more than one role."

"How so?" asked Peter.

Charles offered, "I can see how I was playing two roles at the same time. I was certainly contributing in my role as a schoolteacher. But I found myself consciously trying to get you all to think creatively, *di*vergently, if you will, Dr. Richards, so that the group would use flexible, fluent, and elaborative thinking skills as you had taught us, to take their ideas out of the obvious."

"Okay, I see how I tried to express the community's concerns, but I also see now how I was using the data I was tuned in to, to focus on the implications of the futures we were charged with considering," said Constance.

Anthony broke in. "And you, Pete, knowing you, I'm sure you tried to help the group collaborate toward what you had to do."

Peter said, "You know me too well, Anthony. Collaborative leadership is the only way to get elected, to get a group to honor each other's ideas, to get anything truly done."

"So," said Ellen. "Everyone's truest value was not only representing a group's point of view, but also creating an environment in which we used a variety of skills that made for a think tank that not only thought, but was also productive."

Richards nodded. "You're giving me too much credit. The effectiveness of the group was and is the sum of the coalescence of the collaboration."

Anthony whistled. "Well, that's a mouthful."

The committee had gone home for the evening, save the principal planning team. It was clear they were exhausted.

Principal Smith said it for everyone. "Well, that took ten pounds out of my thinking processes. You're certainly right, Dr. Richards, when you say that we all would rather think fast instead of slow."

Ellen added, "Yes, but any way you look at it, the futures they generated would never have seen the light of day without engaging that process."

"Stepping back and reflecting, as I look at these matrix charts on the easels around us now, there are futures on display that we might never have realized were not only possible, but also probable that we'd never considered," offered Carol.

"I know we had generated purpose," said Mike, "but I can't help thinking that we might have to revisit the purpose we agreed to." He read it aloud. "'*The ABC FFIG recognizes that our school is committed to its obligation to continuously upgrade the capacity of its teaching and learning by using social media to promote interactivity and critical thinking as our prime academic goal. At the same time, this committee recognizes and is committed to practicing safe and positive practices of social media among its stakeholders.*' That's a mouthful, and it really amounts to two purposes, doesn't it?"

John supported the point. "I agree, Mike. We should likely double back on this, if not to synthesize the dual purposes, but also to clarify them."

"I agree, as well," said Richards. "We can do that. Likely it will evolve as we move to the next phase, Scenario Development. In fact, I am sure of it."

"True enough, but again, I do marvel at the quality of their thinking. And I also think it is important to remember that we helped the group learn a whole process, Creative Problem Solving, including a spectrum of creativity techniques. We also accented the need for mastery of futuring, systems disciplines awareness, and collaboration," said Smith.

"And what was truly important was how we were able, as best we could, to create subgroups that represented a cross-section of the stakeholders," said Ellen.

"Yes, but accounting for their skill sets was the secret sauce in the recipe," said Carol.

"Really?" Richards smiled. "How so, do you think?"

"I'll take a stab at that. Let's think a bit. We had Collaborative Leadership specialists. We had creative thinkers, futurists, systems thinkers, and culture experts in various degrees," Mike offered.

"And these really account for the variables we identified within the whole premise of futures-based leadership!" concluded John. "Well, what we did certainly reflected what we want our culture to be able to do."

Richards smiled.

Chapters 5 and 6 described how Phase Two, If-Then Thinking activities, combine to demonstrate how futuring techniques like Futures Wheels and Cross Impact Matrix construction elevate both individuals' and groups' thinking, and perhaps most importantly, dispositions, to generate perspectives that had been developed from Phase One, the Information Gathering segment. The group, armed with new skills sets, competencies, and frames of mind, begins to coalesce around their collective presencing, per Scharmer, to recognize deep purpose and to move up the right side of his Theory U model, toward prototyping and inventing.

We saw evidence of all of the variables within the futures-based change leadership theme: i.e., cultural capacity necessities of systems disciplines' awareness, creative/design thinking, and collaborative leadership, all enhanced via futuring techniques, to zero to numbers of probable futures that appear more likely to emerge as they consider their assigned charge.

On the one hand, it might be enough for an external and/or an internal facilitator to stop group deliberations at this point in order to leapfrog to an action design to meet their agreed-to purpose. Doing this avoids what might be called "Futuring Fatigue."

As was noted in the dialogue and alluded to throughout the book to date, per Daniel Kahneman, where "thinking fast" is the preferred way most people consider issues, "thinking slow" is hard work. Therefore, depending on the issue(s) a group has been undertaking, it might be all right to skip the third phase, Scenario Development, to bring closure. The probable future that decision likely suggests would be an action design product that might not reflect the best of what they have generated to that point, especially if their purpose, as in the case of the example dialogue offered in this book, is still a work in progress.

The recommendation here is that prospective futures-based change leaders *do* use the Phase Three Scenario Development segment. Obviously, the process will take a bit longer, but the payoff will be to everyone's advantage. Developing scenarios that have synthesized from their having pinpointed their emerging futures will evoke not only an intellectual/rational reaction to their likely futures, but will also prompt a more visceral decision process that will prompt their choices to accept, adapt, avoid, or transform the futures they recognize. Moreover, you will have engrained cultural practices that represent new basic assumptions and beliefs. One of these would be that their future is not necessarily imposed on them. Rather, they have choices they can make to more nearly align with their purpose-based futures.

The decision model below captures the point: Where a decision occasion occurs, it is existentially natural for decision makers to identify their choices, presumably grounded in a goal, along with the future for the likely outcomes of each choice, and then to choose one. That choice may have intellectual basis (hopefully). However, it will also reflect the values and emotions of the sum of the individuals involved in that decision.

Returning to the "choose but choose wisely" advice cited several times in this book, the most effective and accepted choice will be one

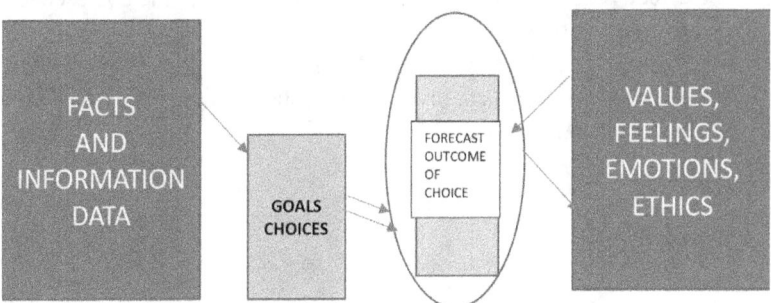

Figure 7.2.

that aligns with the values and feelings of the Whole and is tuned to futures-based outcomes the group has projected as preferable. The activities within the Scenario development phase in the next chapter will do that.

ISSUES TO CONSIDER

To what extent does your school organization:

- Value creative thinking?
- Have the futuring skills to force-fit probable futures?
- Listen to each other?
- Connect creativity to purpose construction?

ESSENTIAL POINTS

1. Creative Problem Solving/Theory U Thinking is neither customarily nurtured nor encouraged in school improvement groups.
2. Groups need to be made aware of the differences between divergent and convergent thinking.
3. Groups need to be aware about how each can complement the other and lead to creative solutions that will work.
4. Cross Impact Matrix thinking enables participants to take probable futures generated by Futures Wheels and to "force-fit" their potential impacts on the task to scrape down deeper at the implications of their ideas.
5. The effectiveness of the group was and is the sum of the coalescence of the collaboration.
6. When group members use their "thinking-specialties"—e.g., decision making, futuring, creativity, and systems thinking—the puzzle pieces come together.

Chapter Eight

Creating Scenarios

"Now we connect the dots," said Dr. Richards.

"Meaning?" asked Carol.

"Meaning," he said, "that we connect the dots, not only to see the whole picture, but to create our own picture of what should be."

Ellen smiled. "Why do I get the idea that our hair is going to hurt again?"

"Yes, it will," said Richards. "We are going to create stories."

"If I understand this process, we are moving to scenario development here, aren't we?" Smith said.

Mike offered his expected yes-buts. "Are we sure we want to try this phase? Our committee is mostly volunteers, and they have worked very hard to tackle what has become a two-headed problem set. If we stretch the process out much more, we might begin to lose some of them."

"'Two-headed'?" asked John.

"Well, sure," offered Ellen. "Our mission at first was to somehow get our arms around a social media policy that would mitigate the social and emotional furor the students were caught in. That was vibrating across the school—behaviorally, emotionally, and academically, too."

Carol agreed. "Yes, and then we morphed toward keeping our focus on those issues while also recognizing that we needed a broader policy approach to how or whether our faculty could use social media in their instruction. It has been an interesting process, but maybe Mike is right. Maybe we've asked enough of the committee members who likely are suffering from a large dose of Futuring Fatigue."

Smith looked at Richards. "What say you, sir?"

"Trace your journey backward before you carve it forward. You came through a very productive and informative Data Gathering Phase. Not only did the committee acquire a lot of information, but they also pieced it together in new ways—newer patterns, more importantly—and some unforeseen tentative conclusions."

"That went pretty well," said Mike.

Carol agreed. "Yes, I really liked the last segment we just came through. Lots of if-thens, lots of futures with a plural, that we might not have considered without having used those futuring skills."

"Especially the Cross-Impact Matrices," John offered. "Then we squeezed those multi-futures and can now see that there are many probable ones that need to be both in our telescope *and* our microscope."

"Nicely put, folks. So, you're satisfied with our futuring and feel like you can now settle into action designing?" asked Principal Smith.

"I have to say, I'm not ready to do that. I think it would be premature. We might find some quick-fix archetypal solutions, so-called, but an impatient, on-to-the-next-issue mindset would result in really bad decision making."

John chimed in. "Without over-philosophizing, were we to stop now"—he made an air quotes sign—"and declare 'victory,' it would be like we in educational leadership do in far too many things—we would short-circuit it."

Carol agreed. "We'd be thinking—what is it called, Dr. Richards?—operationally instead of strategically?"

Principal Smith nodded. "For sure. It's the pinball mindset."

Mike was intrigued. "'Pinball'?"

Smith answered, "Well, the analogy might escape some of you younger ones. But we old-timers actually remember something called pinball machines, and no, not the ones you might play on your tablet. In real pinball, you played a machine that used a spring mechanism to propel a metal ball up a chute and onto a bigger playing board. There were little what we called 'bumpers' that you could manipulate to flick the ball up to other bumpers, where you scored points. The object was to anticipate where the ball might fall and use your 'futures,' your bumper arms, to continue the game.

"It was fun," he added. "A nice combination of short-term anticipation and action."

Creating Scenarios 67

"So," said John, "the thinking, as you say, was short term, and often reactive. Sort of like the legislation that we must obey, where we submit short-term, one-year operational budgetary planning for community approval, from one bumper to the other, with only a vague idea of how to keep that ball from dropping to the bottom."

"And that mindset chain is what we lug around like Marley's ghost," said Smith.

"Okay, we recognize that we need yet to *develop more capacity* of our group to go even deeper," said Ellen. "And the way to do that is to write stories. You say, Dr. Richards, to write 'scenarios'?"

Richards nodded. "That's right. Let me give you an overview of what we need to do in order to take this to the next place. First, I will work a group dialogue where they can ground, more or less, to the probable, emerging futures that their thinking has boiled down to."

"That shouldn't be too difficult," offered Carol.

"I hope so," said Dr. Richards. "It will make the next phase easier, because now we go to Three-Dimensional Futuring."

"So, what we've been doing so far has been two-dimensional," said Mike. "Those 'if-thens' you talk about, some of them were pretty complex, not necessarily just two-dimensional."

"Of course, you are right," Richards responded. "The difference now is that we use the momentum of that kind of thinking to capture as much of the nuances and unexpected ideas, elaborate on the fuller picture, and go three-dimensional, as it were. First, I will model a deceptively simple graphic model. It will look like this." (See Fig 8.1, p. 68.)

The group looked it over.

"Oops, I feel my hair hurting again." Ellen smiled.

Dr. Richards was reassuring. "Actually, the model is very helpful in getting the committee to think both convergently and divergently. And this model is actually interesting because it categorizes, that is, it *convergently* squeezes, their thinking."

"But"—Mike broke in with an *aha* moment—"the four frames the chart creates, as you said, are convergent, yet within the quadrants, there is opportunity for divergent thinking because now the groups can write stories based on the frames!"

Ellen was impressed. "Now the English teacher in me kicks in. This approach looks like a great way to spark thinking for sure. So, let me think. If I chose Quadrant I, LOW commitment by stakeholders, but

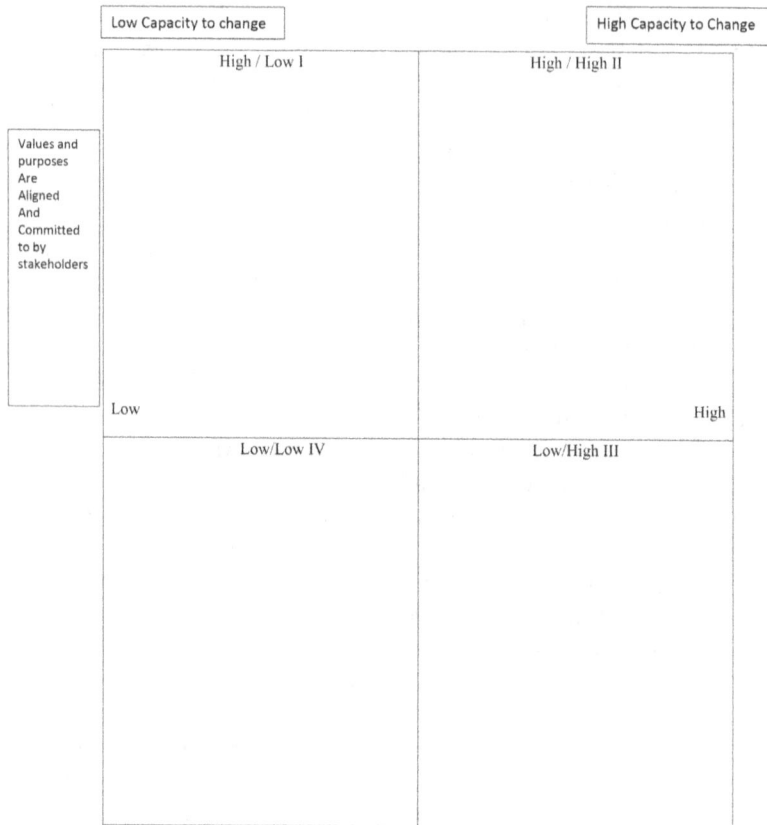

Figure 8.1.

HIGH capacity for change in our school, I'd envision a situation in which I had a school that had the resources and systems to adapt to the issues we have considered in the Information Gathering segments."

"But"—John broke in—"for some reason, our stakeholders, the community, the faculty, even the students, are not very interested in *why* we are considering how social media might be used in instruction and/or for somehow monitoring and controlling how students may or may not use social media."

"That is an unpleasant scenario," said Carol. "We have the way, but we don't have the will."

"And a will without a way suggests ripple effects we would have to consider," said Dr. Smith.

Mike thought aloud. "Then we would have to consider that our efforts would be, at least in the beginning, met with great resistance and doubts. We'd be lucky if any of what we are aiming for would ever succeed."

"Unless we refuse to cave to the resistance," said Dr. Smith. "Clearly that means we have cultural capacity issues anyway, despite having so-called high capacity. That would mean I would have to work harder to build trust and commitment before we go full-on ahead on these changes."

"Well said," agreed Dr. Richards. "Now tell me a story that you can generate from that conclusion."

Ellen began to narrate aloud. ''There was some restlessness as Dr. Smith introduced the new policies that the FFIG committee had created. Science teacher Don jumped up. 'Doc,' he said, 'too much fuss about this social media thing. We have plenty of other issues we need to think about than this. I am a pretty effective teacher, if I don't say so myself, and I don't feel that I or my colleagues have to turn my instruction inside out to formally use social media in my teaching.'

"Others began to murmur, with points for and against. The principal realized this would have to be more carefully explained to the staff. 'I get it,' he said. 'Maybe we are moving too fast. How about I meet with members from each department and provide the necessary staff development to justify effective implementation? I'll send out a plan for this in a few days.'"

John whistled. "Wow, Ellen, that was pretty good. That sounded like a story all right."

"And a likely one, too, with a solution, as well." added Dr. Smith.

"Now, depending on our time needs and on, as you said, 'Futures Fatigue,' the most productive approaches here would be based on any number of presentation formats," Richards pointed out.

"You divide the whole group randomly into four groups, one for each quadrant."

Mike asked, "Does it have to be four?"

Richards was adamant. "More than four gets clumsy. Less than four prematurely squeezes the thinking toward so-called preferable futures. They're not ready for that."

"Okay, so, what is next?" Ellen asked.

"We explain the quadrants to which they are assigned. We let them internally consider what these suggest insofar as what social media policy changes might mean. Then we let them name their team, maybe create a logo," said Richards.

"Then we offer options in demonstrating the scenario that they will present."

"Such as?" asked Smith.

"You encourage some creative, *di*vergent thinking here," said Richards. "Newscasts, skits, newspaper headlines, rhymes, websites, debate-panel dramatizations, videos, whatever they think will most clearly capture and deliver, but one that might just be their Emerging Future, according to their thinking."

"I guess the next piece would be to present them to the other three groups," said Carol. "But how would we know which scenario emerges as the best, the most probable, future?"

"First of all, you emphasize that the scenario they are developing is, in fact, a PROBABLE scenario. That is really important. In other words, it may not necessarily be the one that they personally favor as a preferable one. Instead, it is the one that, by their data analyses and two-dimensional, futuring activities, appears to yield the most likely on-rushing future. Our collective task, after the presentations, becomes choosing which of the presentations best meets the criteria."

"And they are?" wondered Mike.

"There are four," said Dr. Richards. "They are the extent to which they seem *relevant*, *challenging*, *plausible*, and *clear*. These are the same criteria that Adam Kahane uses in his transformative scenario–planning processes on the corporate and international levels. And they certainly have great value in our process, as well, at ABC High School."

This segment has critical themes, advice, and principles to consider. It reviews how the previous process activity segments have summed to a group that has acquired good mastery of futuring skills. This began with a comprehensive information analysis extraction. Their mastery of two-dimensional, if-then futuring strategies—i.e., futures wheels and cross impact matrix exercises—yielded an array of probable, what Scharmer calls "Emerging Futures" (2014). As Ellen pointed out, many of these probable futures would likely not have been noted without having used these strategies. And in doing so, participants' *dispositions* are beginning to change.

In some senses, this development has as much power as the conclusions they are beginning to reach. That is, they are beginning to consider that their own futures mindset can change, especially one that may smack of passivity instead of one that can be more proactive.

With a handful of likely, probable emerging futures now available, the group, under Dr. Richards's guidance, now begins to consider how the two-dimensional ideas can go through a three-dimensional futuring process that will sharpen their futures-based thinking, and as importantly, their decision-actions.

This begins with scenario development. Richards's explanation is based largely on Adam Kahane's work in *Transformative Scenario Planning* (2014). Richards spells out the group preparation and implementation needed to properly enable the committee to execute this part of the stage. It is very important to see how the process winds from convergent to divergent to convergent again, and it ends with his definition of the criteria of worthy scenario presentations:

Relevance illustrates the requirement that whatever the group may have developed within the confines of their quadrant axes clearly pertains to the purpose that the group had distilled to in the Information Phase.

Challenging shows that the group's conclusions dramatize the level of deep thinking they have invested into their "story." They must show, through their presentation, the issues and obstructions that their future story will need to consider.

Plausible requires that the "whole" of what they present, although it may be complex, is nonetheless logical within the levels of complex consideration of its issues and themes. To claim that "the Martians will land and solve our problem" is probably not probable.

Finally, the scenario must be *Clear.* That the scenario presentation is unequivocal is important, because the message cannot be misunderstood.

Now what must be considered is what to do with what is developing:

"Well, that was interesting," said John.

"Yes, it was," said Mike. "They did a great job and got invested in weighing the pros and cons of each presentation."

"Quadrant One went pretty much the way Ellen had envisioned. It started out pretty negative, but then it began to insert ways to make it work against the group's purposes," said Dr. Smith.

"Actually," said Dr. Richards, "in retrospect, I think I let that thinking evolve a little too prematurely. They began to seep over to the next part of the phase. But I didn't want to obstruct their thinking processes. You'll see what I mean when I explain in a bit."

Carol spoke up. "Okay, let me take a crack at the Quadrant Two Team. Before I do, I just want to point out that One's presentation was very novel. the eulogy to the demise of ABC High School was a bit jolting, but it certainly enabled them to get their point across.

"But Quadrant Two," she continued, "also had an interesting spin."

"Their parameters may have been the easiest to factor for," said Ellen. "High Capacity *and* High Will, no less. Using a video of interviews of stakeholders where they enthusiastically embraced the district's choices, and linking them with forward thinking purpose that could count on district prioritizing resources to support the changes, is nirvana for any of us. And it was effectively done."

"Not so for Quadrant Three," demurred John. "As you might expect, since its parameters forced some gloomy projections: LOW Capacity, despite HIGH willingness to make these changes was a 'winner' in the sense that it just seemed so perfectly tuned to criteria requirements."

"Maybe that was why their presentation was so well done," added Dr. Smith. "The website was filled with a variety of links and options to consider as to how this future would play out, dismally I might add, at least in the short term."

"Well, Quadrant Four was the pits, as you might have expected," said Mike. "I was in that group. First, they were very downbeat and unwilling to even try to project what this future might look like. But I have to say that their real estate brochure certainly made a strong case that the ABC community, not to mention our school, would look like a deserted ghost town right quick."

"Now," said Richards, "what did you think of how the whole group vote went?"

That choice is saved for the next chapter, "Adapt or Transform." A group that has been brought through and has chosen to bring themselves through this process and then walked away from their choice at this juncture would be committing a very grievous error, not only from an academic standpoint, but also from an "action" one. The FFIG committee, in our model, is obligated to consider what must be done next. this is no easy choice.

ISSUES TO CONSIDER

To what extent does your school organization:

- See the need to proceed, or to settle on the thinking they have invested to date?
- Distinguish among the probable futures thus developed to synthesize them into four groups?
- Recognize the implications of the quadrants into which they will be assigned?
- Have the objectivity to use the criteria for choosing the most probable future even if it may not be the most preferable one?

ESSENTIAL POINTS

1. Three-dimensional thinking is dependent on two-dimensional thinking.
2. Scenario Building is but one of several three-dimensional processes.
3. Scenario Building builds probable futures, NOT preferable ones.
4. It is helpful to use a Cartesian approach, where four conditions represent the sum of the probable futures that have been developed.
5. Then randomly divide the group into each of the four potential scenarios the format suggests.
6. Next, emphasize that the group is to develop a "story" that fleshes out a probable future that quadrant suggests.
7. After their presentation, use the four criteria provided to identify the most PROBABLE future.

Chapter Nine

A Futures-Based Process in Place
Action Design

Ulysses, the union leader, sighed. "I'm wondering. Why did Dr. Richards show us the ending of Dickens's *A Christmas Carol* at the end of last week's meeting?"

Samantha Student Council agreed. "Yes, and even then, he never commented on it. At least, he hasn't yet. Maybe he will now, since the meeting is starting soon. I'd never seen that movie before."

Ulysses smiled. "As your Advanced Placement English teacher, I guess I took it for granted that you'd studied Dickens in one English class or another. Dickens is one of the preeminent authors in English literature."

"Okay, now it comes back to me," she said. *"A Tale of Two Cities, Great Expectations."*

Patricia, the PTA parent, volunteered, "Well, I had you back in the day, Mr. Joyce. And I've seen that movie many times. I am pretty sure that Dickens ended his novel by showing that Scrooge resolved *to transform* himself away from being an un-mourned miser to becoming a benefactor not only to Cratchit's family, but to all mankind."

John laughed. "That's one way to look at it. I took it to mean that he was still a selfish old coot, more concerned about his so-called memory than his fellow man."

Ulysses was about to applaud the thinking of each when Paul, the school custodian, broke in. "Well, Scrooge could have chosen to change, but maybe more slowly than the book showed. Sort of like what we just argued about in the last meeting, when we agreed that the most probable future we face at ABC High School is seemingly the ability to change our policies about how teachers should use social media in their instruction and how students should use it in school, too. But it was also clear that the willingness was not necessarily there."

"I thought that was a pretty accurate scenario," said the PTA representative. "I know that my parent members had mixed opinions of this from the beginning. I was and still am one of those. I know Dr. Smith has expressed that he intends to work hard to train faculty in how to use social media in our faculty's teaching, and he also said he would ease into this part of the policy as the staff becomes more comfortable with its guidelines.

"But" she continued, "it's also clear that the administration and the staff's ability to control the students' usage will be difficult at best."

It was then that Dr. Smith reconvened the meeting. "Good evening!" exclaimed Principal Smith. "Congratulations on your hard work. We are coming around the bend now, I think. Isn't that right, Dr. Richards?"

Richards stood up. "We are, Dr. Smith. Actually, I was going to take my leave of you tonight, congratulate you on your thinking, and ride out of town."

Ellen was perplexed, to say the least. "Are you sure about that, Dr. Richards? If we stop now—if you leave now—I'm wondering what we actually have accomplished."

Ulysses raised his hand. "If I may, Dr. Smith, methinks that Dr. Richards is testing us. Of course, he knows that we are not done. What we have done, for sure, is identified a Probable Scenario 'winner,' so to speak. But what we do with or against that scenario has not been determined."

Paul agreed. "It is a well-constructed scenario, but keep in mind, the future that it brings is more of the same old, same old. ABC as a district—ABC as a community—will suffer for this probable future."

Mike broke in. "If it is the probable likely future for ABC, I don't know if there is much we can do to avoid it. Isn't that right, Dr. Richards?"

Richards apologized. "No, I am not leaving, unless that is, your futuring fatigue has worn you down so much that you don't see we have more to do, none of which we'd be able to build toward without having worked so hard to get here in the first place.

"Let me collect things for a moment," he went on, "to remind you how you have coalesced as a futures-based think tank, how you used a cross-section of information sources, parsed them, distilled them, and applied them, to enable you to forecast what their sum might mean. That led you to be able to more truly and more substantially narrow things down to probable futures. And that led you to more deeply consider the implications of those probable futures.

"And along the path, you instinctively began to sort these out between what is probable and what is preferable. Finally, or actually, not-so-finally, you've come to this crossroad."

Samantha immediately understood what he meant. "Dr. Richards, as Ellen pointed out, we are not really done. Now we have to figure out whether to accept this future. I for one do *not* accept it. It reminds me of, as Paul pointed out, 'more the same old, same old'. We have the chance…"

Carol completed the sentence, "…to transform. Frankly, ABC has always sought a minimum of changes. We are almost always satisfied to accept the same old, same old, to turn the thermostat maybe just a little, but never to seek to be more than what we can be."

Mike disagreed. "You know, all this is well and good. I will remind you that when Dr. Smith brought this group together—if I may speak for you, Dr. Smith—I do not think you meant to turn the world upside down. You charged this group with formulating workable, effective policies for students' use of social media. That evolved to using social media in the classroom.

"Now," he went on, "I get the idea that we have broken into altogether new territory. And maybe we have exceeded our boundaries by choosing what kind of actions we should take after we have zeroed in on the probable future."

The group murmur escalated. It seemed there were strong feelings on all sides of the conversation. Dr. Smith looked at Dr. Richards. "Do you want to take this, or should I?"

Richards was adamant. "This is your school. You need to help them get over this hurdle."

Smith nodded. "Of course. Few people more nearly believe in collaborative leadership than I do. However, situationally, this calls for me to bring structure to their thinking."

He stood, and the group immediately began to quiet. He smiled. "I think it's necessary for me to answer Mike's question. And the answer is, I am perfectly happy to let the world reasonably turn upside down.

For sure, ABC on the whole could use some transformation. Someone said, 'When you stop trying to get better, you stop being good.' And actually, these several months of analysis and exchange have been downright invigorating. Wasn't it wonderful to see this kind of high engagement? To hear so many creative ideas? To watch actual futuring skills evolve? For me, it was my personal Preferable Future that our futuring about social media would become a metaphor for our overall futuring for ABC. I am pleased it has come to that, and I am doubly glad that our student council president was the one to first reject adapting to our probable, *unpreferable* future in favor of something with more power to transform who and what we are. Dr. Richards?"

Richards stood. "It's great that the team learning has converted you all to edu-futurists. Would that more schools had the experiences and training that you have taken yourselves through. In a sense, though, I *was* ready to ride out of town. Our goal was to help you co-develop capacity and leverage futuring strategies to create a new Whole. You are well on the way to doing just that."

John spoke. "We all appreciate that, Dr. Richards. Do you and Dr. Smith agree that we have the capacity to go forward?"

"You do," answered Richards, "but you have decisions to make. Do you mean to adapt to the future you foresee, or do you mean to transform away from it?"

"Again, that depends on the dispositions of our leadership," answered Mike. "Dr. Smith, I heard loud and clear that you are anxious to go forward on the transformational level. I'm game if you are. But does the collective will of this group have the dispositions, too, in addition to the skill sets, to engage that sort of commitment?"

Carol spoke up. "I'm comfortable with both our skill sets, of course with continued guidance, *and* with our dispositions to move forward. You're right, though, Mike. Now we are in Theory U and in Collaborative Leadership, not to mention the Shared Vision dimensions, of what we have done. It's time to see if we have circled our wagons around our coalesced intentions."

"After all," Ellen offered, "energy follows attention."

The group, having heard that quote more than once, good-naturedly groaned.

Dr. Richards smiled. "You are even recognizing how the skill sets twine a round each other!"

"Yes, you 'teached' us good!" Ulysses, the English teacher, smiled.
"I guess that means we are developing cultural capacity."
"It does," Smith said. "And now it is up to how we collectively see ourselves both from the fifty-thousand-feet level, and individually, to decide whether we adapt or transform."
"I'm not sure what you are driving at," said Patricia.
"The words seem obvious enough," said Al, the social studies teacher. "To 'adapt' means that we have to settle for, accept, what we think is and will be. It means that we work *with* the future that we think is most probable. It means that we believe, practically speaking, that we *must* live it with, because we either don't have the will to move away from it or that its roots are too hard to remove from our souls."
"And to 'transform' means to change completely, restructure, redo, re-create to the future that we think best meets our long-range purpose," volunteered Samantha. "I've already told you what my position is."
"Before we finalize our choice, let's try one more analysis," said Dr. Richards. "I am going to redivide you randomly and give you several minutes to analyze the two choices before you. Ask yourselves, 'What are the pluses of adapting? Of transforming? What are the minuses?' Most importantly, what would be interesting to pursue in either of the two choices?"

That Richards gave additional time to the teams to revisit the two choices might seem like overkill. However, the choice they are about to make has much significance. On the one hand, their journey to this decision pivot point is textbook-like exemplary: They have engaged each other and the themes, issues, data, and probabilities from numerous angles that might never have occurred to them at the outset. They have scraped away at obstructing mindsets, used new skills, and acquired new dispositions that place themselves in position to make this choice.

On the other, and perhaps more important, hand, no matter whether they choose to adapt or to transform, *they* have transformed into a think-tank team with the capacity to join with their principal to co-empower toward preferable futures in any venue.

Richards reconvened the groups into a Whole. "Let's distill what each group has decided. Before we do that, we need consensus on this decision. However, we are also not going to belabor it. As I gauge the groups' input, I reserve the right to declare consensus if the *great* majority of the groups indicate that they are in one camp or another. Group One, what say you?"

Carol stood up. "I must say, this was a tough one. I have to tell you that I held out hard for 'Transform' in our group. Maybe the rest of my group colleagues are more practical than I am. They saw 'Adapt' as the preferable approach."

Paul raised his hand from within his group. "I chose 'Adapt' from this same group. I greatly, greatly respect Carol's zeal and her intent. But we, the rest of us, quite frankly, doubted that we have the time to totally redo what we are as ABC. Better, we thought, to tweak our guidelines and policies, and react and adjust as the situations present themselves, than to look too far down the road."

"Group Two?" asked Dr. Richards.

Mike stood up. "Well, I have been the Futures Grinch from the beginning of this whole journey. But I have drunk the Kool-Aid, along with the rest of us. We know that it will be far more difficult than choosing to adapt, but we think to transform is the only way to go. We have come too far to accept reaction when we now realize that we *do* have it within us to proact to futures we not only prefer, but that we also know are in the best projected interests of our students and our community across time."

Businessperson Barry stood up. "Well, the Ts have it. We, in this group, out of deep concerns for the community as well as for the ABC School, not only now, but for our projected futures, decided on the need to seek transformation, too. As a community businessperson here for many years, I can attest to how private businesses too often just blow away in the face of winds that they should have prepared for. We all did a lot of work considering the economic, civic, and demographic trends and themes that we cannot avoid. We realize the responsibility—actually we are awed by it. But we are committed to doing what is necessary."

"Transform, it is," declared the principal. "However, we do not ignore the fact that some of you see a slower and less ambitious plan as a better decision. I can promise you that we will listen to your cautions and factor them into the plan we are going to co-design."

The group adjourned, actually to the local diner, to celebrate their hard work and to debrief among themselves. However, not everyone went to the diner. The original think tank reconvened to Dr. Smith's office.

Smith was pleased; they all appeared to be. However, they were also both weary and wary. John said it best: "More work for Mother."

Richards laughed. "Now there are two basic developments to accommodate. At first, they will seem to be at odds, but actually they very much complement each other. Each has its role. I will leave it to you to decide about that."

"Don't keep us in suspense, Dr. Richards. What are they?" asked Ellen.

He went on, "One is *in*organic, and the other is its opposite. *In*organic speaks to the need to craft and produce a formal, hard-copy design plan."

"Like the ones in loose-leaf binders behind every leader's desk?" asked Ellen.

Richards laughed. "Yes, I'm afraid so. Like the ones that, let's say, an accrediting agency requires. You know, the agencies that detail the goals and expectations, the strategies you will use, the ways you would measure the success of meeting those goals."

"Sounds like you're apologizing for this," John said.

"I guess I tip off my preference in favor of the 'organic' approach," said Richards. "The *in*organic plans sometimes smack of a rigid formality that often stifles the plan's intent. The boxes and squares templates, the due dates, and the criteria measurements imply an artificiality to the whole plan, and maybe that's why you can often write your name on the dust these binders harvest on those principals' shelves."

"Yet at the same time, Dr. Richards," said the principal, "these are necessary, aren't they? That they are there sends a message of our intent. They assure the governance teams and accrediting agencies that much thought has been invested, and that adherence to the plan will yield good results."

Richards nodded. "Yes, you are right. And you will need one for certain."

Carol anticipated the next point. "And then there is 'organic'," she offered. "I think that is more difficult to define, isn't it?"

Richards nodded. "Supreme Court Justice Potter Stewart, when he was asked to define 'pornography,' once said, 'I shall not today attempt further to define the kinds of material I understand to be embraced within that shorthand description ["hard-core pornography"], and perhaps I could never succeed in intelligibly doing so. But *I know it when I see it*....' For me, I frankly find defining 'organic' insofar as action design also difficult to define. But I know it when I see it."

"I do know that I, and that all of you, can spot it when it presents itself while the group begins to plan together. In fact, you have seen organic thinking throughout the futuring process. You saw it when an idea popped up out of the blue. You saw it when two individuals, first at odds, suddenly 'saw the Theory U light' and coalesced their thinking into something altogether new.

"What is really fascinating is what we haven't seen yet, if we have done our process correctly, where the sum of the team learning and personal mastery that has permeated the team *creates new futures*. These will occur well after a plan is put on paper. Often, it will occur when you least expect it. In fact, it is almost impossible to force these new ideas, new and creative decisions, new dispositions, to emerge until the conditions, the ecology of the group, nurtures it into existence."

Mike whistled. "Well, that is downright poetic, Dr. Richards, and just as profound. Maybe I can offer another metaphor from my biology teaching days? A healthy pond is a balanced array of subsystems, where the combination of their presence aligns with each other so that the whole pond can thrive. It is natural; it is organic."

"So, the reason my orchid looks more dead than alive is because I have it in the wrong window?" joked Carol. "Because the conditions for its existence are faulty."

"And now," offered Dr. Smith, "we see the power of the organic as the true, deep, purpose-based, long-lasting energy source necessary for assuring a sustainable future. A preferred one."

John thought aloud. "Great thinking. But now I am wondering, what do we do next?"

"I have some suggestions," said Richards. "We can emphasize one over the other, even skip some as the plan evolves. But basically, we begin by distinguishing between the two kinds of plans and then offer a template that is formal in appearance but leaves a measure of fluidity in it to allow for organic thinking to have room to flourish along the way." He produced a template. "Take a look at this inorganic template."

Table 9.1.

GOAL	STRATEGIES	PERSON RESPONSIBLE	TIMETABLE	OBSTRUCTIONS	RESOURCES	CRITERIA FOR SUCCESS

John commented, "It's pretty straightforward. Pretty much what most state education department charts expect, or accrediting agencies, or grant applications."

Richards agreed. "Yes, hence my *in*organic label. I have some guidelines. For example, the Goal column really only has one goal, one BIG idea, that captures the deepest purpose the team has generated.

"Following from that," he continued, "are strategies, ideas that in some sort of sequence will combine to ensure that goal is met.

"Now, hear me on this. It's my firm belief that the plan creators skip over the interior columns—the who, the when, the obstructions, the resource columns—for the moment. While they, too, deserve their share of futures-based thinking, it is that last column that wags the inorganic dog."

Mike spoke first. "I'd call it the Accountability Column."

"And you'd be right," replied Richards. "I suspect that that term might put some of the plan creators off."

"But it is necessary," said Dr. Smith. "It's quite frankly, politically inescapable. However, far more importantly, *far* more importantly, creating the criteria for success, both for the overall BIG IDEA, and for the strategies that support it, sends three messages at least: One is the political one, and in my mind, an essential but the least important message; another is that we all need to be commonly clear on how we can link the BIG IDEA and the strategies, to determine whether they are aligned and effective."

"And the third?" asked Mike.

"The third," he said, "is that we must establish *multiple* criteria for assessing a strategy's effectiveness! The word itself, 'criteria', is plural. That is to say, that the strategies' complexity and the ambition the team plan creators will generate, of their nature, will require several multidimensional ways to perceive their value."

"I'd suggest that we concentrate on the *in*organic template completion for now, as a structure, a framework to kick-start the thinking but only after the team planning creators remind themselves of the purposes they had generated when we began this journey," said the principal.

"You mean the BIG IDEAS, the themes that have been before us since we began this journey?" asked Mike.

"I do," said Smith. "I believe that affirming the BIG IDEAS from the outset will lay acorns to leave room for the organic thinking that Dr. Smith has described."

Smith looked to Dr. Richards. He nodded. "Yes, I think that is the best way to go. But first let me remind you about some managerial leadership issues to keep in mind:
"Decide if your culture is ready for your plan. Ask yourselves if the capacities you sought to nurture are in place."

"In this case, you are referring to Collaborative Leadership, to Systems Disciplines, and to Theory U/Design Thinking skills," said Carol. "I am pretty comfortable with the presence of these skills myself. You can see their operation in the ideas and opinions the teams have expressed."

"I agree," said Dr. Richards.

He continued, "Another consideration is that you are satisfied with the futuring skills and more importantly, the futuring dispositions they have applied to the tasks."

"No problem there," said John. "They did great work with the forecasting skills and with their scenario development."

"And they dispassionately homed in on the Probable Emerging Future," offered Ellen. "That speaks to the existence of their dispositions."

Dr. Richards continued, "We wouldn't be practicing what we preach if we didn't consider possible and perhaps even probable futures that may obstruct the design planning at this stage. There are several, and we have considered these along the way, I believe."

"Such as?" asked Mike.

"Rather than look to Dr. Richards for these 'yes-buts,' why not have us generate what we might have to contend with?" said the principal. "It will sharpen our own futuring skills."

John spoke first. "Some might feel that we realistically don't have the resources to invest toward a deep-purpose transformational, long-term plan."

Mike offered, "I can see that as a likely yes-but, and it deserves its time in the sun, because if isn't discussed, it may very well be the elephant in the room."

John agreed. "For sure. But I also feel that the skills we have developed—the creative thinking, the purpose generation, the futuring, and the collaborative energies of a cross-section of the community—will organically respond to that point."

"Something else to think about," said Ellen, "is asking everyone to widen their definition of resources away from merely money. We will need to keep spending money issues before us, but money is not the only resource."

"There's expertise, there's time, there's creative thinking, and there's will itself," offered Carol. "In the end, and often organically, as you pointed out, Dr. Richards, where folks recognize that 'necessity is indeed the mother of invention' solutions to what you need to co-generate."

"So clearly, as Ellen pointed out, we cannot ignore the probability, but we certainly cannot let our mindsets about resources immobilize us," said Dr. Smith.

"Okay, here's another," said Ellen. "I've seen too many groups at ABC eagerly tackle an issue, only to become disillusioned along the way. Sometimes it's because the mission or purpose they were assigned to work on was blurry. Sometimes it was because they didn't have the capacity to do anything meaningful. And other times, outside forces would not accept what they offered, out of political reasons or otherwise."

Carol vigorously agreed. "I've seen that happen far too many times, really for the reasons that Ellen cited. If only the parameters for the decision-action were laid out in the beginning. If only the members had been shown they have the skills and dispositions developed. And by the way, I do think that we have taken care of that red flag."

Richards agreed. "Yes, and what you speak to is *trust*. That lies at the bottom of any triangle that shows how a team can be effective. If the issues you cite are not addressed from the outset, and as importantly, not revisited when one sees trust violated, all will topple."

"I am sure other ideas about possible and probable obstructions to our mission may arise. I am going to have my technology department create a website with a forum feature that I will take personal responsibility for, seeing to it that whatever issues arise and are posted there are answered by me. I will also tell you, that while the Board of Education is my boss, they have authorized me to see this through without interference, and see this through I will," Smith declared.

Richards brought closure. "Okay, I will post a calendar for how the process will proceed. The first meeting will be organizational. Then we can split up, perhaps meeting electronically, to rough out the tasks assigned and to create a Futures Forward for Social Media plan."

"Let's saddle up," said Dr. Smith.

A Futures-Based Process in Place

ISSUES TO CONSIDER

To what extent does your school organization:

- Connect its cultural beliefs with its decision to adapt or transform?
- Determine the differences in its evolution according to the processes it has mastered?
- Have the collaborative leadership practices, systems disciplines' mastery, Theory U thinking, futures dispositions, and forecasting skills to embed an action design that meets the purposes it has generated?

ESSENTIAL POINTS

1. A process as depicted, done correctly, transforms a culture and embeds new kinds of thinking into its practices.
2. It typically changes their dispositions about futuring and change.
3. However, it does not necessarily inspire a group to transform.
4. They might, for a variety of reasons, opt to adapt instead of transform.
5. As with convergent and divergent thinking, there is a difference between the organic and inorganic planning action design.
6. However, they both complement each other. The facilitator needs to be conscious of each's existence in the design process
7. Planning for the action design phase is a recursive dependent on the mastery of the process skills and dispositional changes that preceded it.

References

Bernato, Richard. 2017. *Futures-Based Change Leadership.* Rowan and Littlefield, Maryland.
Collins, Jim. 2001. *From Good to Great.* New York: Harper Collins.
Covey, Steven. 1989. *The Seven Habits of Effective People.* New York: Simon and Schuster.
Diamandis, Peter H., and Kotler, Steven. 2020. *The Future Is Happening Faster Than You Think.* New York: Simon and Schuster. Kindle Edition.
Kahane, Adam. 2014. *Transformative Scenario Planning.* San Francisco: Brett-Koehler. Kindle Edition.
Kahneman, Daniel. 2011. *Thinking Fast and Slow.* New York: Farrar, Straus and Giroux. Kindle Edition.
La Loux, Frederic. 2014. *Reinventing Organizations: A Guide to Creating Organizations Inspired by the Next Stage of Human Consciousness.* Belgium: Nelson Parker. Kindle Edition.
Lencioni, Patrick. 2010. *The Five Dysfunctions of a Team.* San Francisco: Jossey-Bass.
Muls, Jael et al. July 22, 2019. "Identifying the nature of social media policies in high schools." *Education and Information Technologies*, (25) 281–305.
Otchie, W.O., and Pedaste, M. 2020. "Using social media for learning in high schools: A systematic literature review." *European Journal of Educational Research*, 9(2), 889–903. https://doi.org/10.12973/eu-jer.9.2.889.
Raellin, Joseph. 2016. "Imagine There Are No Leaders: Reframing Leadership as Collaborative Agency." *Leadership*, 12(2), 131–58. Accessed October 10, 2015.
Senge, Peter, Otto Scharmer, Joseph Jaworski, and Betty Sue Flowers. 2004. *Presence.* New York: Doubleday.

Senge, Peter, and eds. 2016. *Schools That Learn*. New York: Doubleday. Kindle Edition.
Scharmer, Otto. 2014. *Leading from the Emerging Future*. San Francisco: Barrett-Koehler. Kindle Edition.
Scharmer, Otto. 2015. *The Theory U*. San Francisco: Barrett-Koehler.
Webb, Amy. 2016. *The Signals Are Talking*. New York: Perseus Books.
Wohlsetter, Priscilla et al. 1994. *School Based Management: Organizing for High Involvement*. San Francisco: Jossey-Bass.
Wang, Yinying. 2013. "Social Media in Schools: A Treasure Trove or Hot Potato?" Educational Policy Studies Faculty Publications. 18. https://scholarworks.gsu.edu/eps_facpub/18.

About the Author

The sum of **Richard Bernato** is commitment to re-creating education, instructionally and organizationally, so that it engages all who serve youngsters to develop new capacities to meet not only the emerging, probable and preferred, but also the *projected* futures that await us. Doing so more nearly ensures a future where all mankind can benefit from the fruits of a universally empowered world. His plus-fifty-year career includes leadership and catalytic roles from the pre-K through doctoral preparation levels. It is complemented by publications, curriculum and simulations projects, consulting, webinars, and books, all intended to prompt transformation wherever it can take place.

www.ingramcontent.com/pod-product-compliance
Lightning Source LLC
Chambersburg PA
CBHW071851230426
43671CB00012B/2145